# MAKE THE CLARITY CALL TO YOURSELF

Enhance Your Self-Awareness
Bring the Best Version of You
Unlock Limitless Productivity
Thrive in Abundance

**AMI RASHEED**
Life Clarity Coach

Clever Fox® PUBLISHING
Chennai • Bangalore

CLEVER FOX PUBLISHING
Chennai, India

Published by CLEVER FOX PUBLISHING 2025

ISBN: 978-93-6707-835-8

# Dedication

I humbly dedicate this work to you, my readers.

# CONTENTS

# FOREWORD

There's a moment in every leader's life when the world goes silent—not around them, but within them. That moment, if embraced, becomes the turning point. It's the moment you call yourself for a real, raw, and honest conversation. And that is exactly what this book does—it gives you the courage, the language, and the clarity to answer that call.

Ami Rasheed is not just one of my brightest students—she is a living example of what happens when a confused mind dares to seek clarity. From dusty village dreams to Dubai's shining skyline, from silent classrooms to stage-worthy presence, her story isn't one of shortcuts. It's a story of searching, stumbling, standing again, and then soaring—with purpose.

She didn't write this book just to impress you. She wrote it to *ignite* you. Every chapter in this book will make you pause, reflect, and ask yourself one powerful question:

**"Am I really clear about where I'm going?"**

If the answer is "no" or "not sure," then *Make the Clarity Call to Yourself* is not a book—it's your compass.

What I love the most is how Ami blends storytelling, self-awareness, leadership, and spirituality in a way even a fifth grader can understand, but a CEO will still find profound. That's the magic of this work. Simplicity with depth. Realness with strategy. Vision with action.

The metaphors she uses—like the dusty prism and the spectrum of light—are more than beautiful. They are unforgettable.

She teaches you how to dust off your mind, refocus your lens, and unlock the vibrant potential hiding inside you.

This is not a book to finish. It's a book to start with.

Start with your *clarity* call. Answer it with intention. Read it with your journal by your side. And take action with your future self in mind.

I am proud not just of the book Ami has written, but of the person she has become. She took her pain and turned it into power. She took confusion and carved out clarity—not just for herself, but for the thousands this book will touch.

Let this book be your turning point.

Let this book be the mirror you need.

And if you ever feel lost again—remember what Ami reminds us: *Clarity is not a destination. It's your daily decision.*

With respect and belief in your journey,

**Farookh Sensei**
*Leadership Mastercoach & Internal Ignitor*
*Author | Speaker | Mentor to Mentors*

# ACKNOWLEDGEMENTS

Without gratitude, this book would be incomplete. To Rasheed Palliyalil, my friend and partner in this journey, thank you for being my writing mentor and greatest support system. You went through my thoughts and drafts multiple times, offered resources I needed for research, and gave me the space and freedom, despite family responsibilities, to travel and explore whatever my writing demanded. Without you, this book would not have been possible.

To Noura and Uday, my biggest cheerleaders, thank you for typing out my thoughts, editing my earliest drafts, and standing by me with complete trust. You believed in me before this book even took shape.

My heartfelt thanks to Farookh Sensei, my mentor and internal ignitor, who first recognized the spark in my writing. His belief in my potential ignited the idea for this book. Through his mentorship, I've grown in ways I never imagined. I continue to rely deeply on his thoughts, insights, and unwavering guidance.

Forever grateful to my parents, for giving me a life, love and care. Your foundation and values made everything possible in my life.

Thank you, Manoj Vasudevan, Toastmasters World Champion of Public Speaking, for standing by me throughout this journey, from the initial inspiration to the final stages and beyond.

Thank you, Muneer Amayoor, Amazon best selling author and radio presenter for reading through the entire first version of my manuscript and offering valuable insights. It enabled me to clearly identify the gaps. Your mentorship throughout this publishing journey, including guidance on becoming an Amazon bestseller, has been invaluable.

To Farook Sensei's Ledge team, your consistent encouragement and those enthusiastic thumbs-ups on my posts, motivated me to keep sharing and creating. A special thanks to Mamta Joshi, a poet for patiently listening as I bounced off ideas often through our WhatsApp chats, and to Safa Majeed, Founder of communication training company Cvox360, for recemmondations when I needed direction the most. Safa's guidance made all the difference.

To Mitreyi Venugopal, your dedicated editorial support during your studies meant the world to me. Despite your academic workload, you made time to work through this manuscript with me, multiple times. I was deeply moved when you told me how the book helped you prioritize, visualize, and even inspired you to put up a wallpaper of your goals. When you topped your university, you said this book played a vital role, and to me, that is the most powerful testament to its purpose. I owe you for being part of this journey with such heart. A heartfelt thank you to my incredible publishing team at Clever Fox.

Thank you, Moinudheen Palliyalil, my brother, for providing the diagrams for this book. Your contribution brought my words to life visually.

I also extend my gratitude to the podcasters, YouTubers, and workshop facilitators whose wisdom and insights have deeply influenced this book. Visionaries like John Assaraf, Niurka, Jack Canfield, Lisa Nichols, Vishen Lakhiani, Brian Tracy, John Maxwell, and countless other leaders have been invaluable sources of inspiration. I am forever grateful for the generous endorsement from leader Jack Canfield, along with leaders Patty and Earl Waud, my valued learning partner.

Special thanks to Earl Waud for his AI workshops and guidance on book publishing, and connecting me with leader Jack, which greatly supported my journey.

To everyone who played a role, in my journey, whether mentioned here or not, know that your impact lives in these pages. Words are not enough to express my gratitude.

## Why Great Leaders Recommend This Book?

*"Ami Rasheed's Make the Clarity Call to Yourself is an inspiring and practical guide to living with purpose and intention. Through personal stories and actionable strategies, Ami empowers readers to cut through the noise, discover their inner truth, and create a life aligned with their highest potential. If you're ready to transform confusion into clarity and dreams into results, this is the book to start with."*

**— Jack Canfield,**
**Coauthor of Chicken Soup**
**for the Soul® and The Success Principles™**

*"In this thought-provoking book, Ami Rasheed explores how we can program our minds to develop the clarity we need to decide on the best course of action in any situation. It provides actionable strategies, habits, and exercises, which makes it an essential reading for anyone seeking greater clarity."*

**— Manoj Vasudevan,**
**World Champion of Public Speaking 2017, Next Level Leadership Readiness Expert & Author**

*"Let's face it, clarity doesn't just show up one day. It's something we create through reflection, intention, and aligned action. Ami Rasheed understands this deeply, and Make the Clarity Call to Yourself gives you the tools*

*to do exactly that. It's an inspiring, practical, and heartfelt guide for anyone ready to step into their best life."*

**— Patty Aubery,**
**#1 New York Times best-selling author**
**Author of Chicken Soup for the Working Woman's Soul® and Past President of Chicken Soup for the Soul® Enterprises, Inc.**

*"In the noise of the world, your true voice can become a whisper. But it is still there, waiting. 'Clarity Call' is the echo that reminds you to listen. Ami Rasheed's words will guide you back to that voice… and when you hear it, everything shifts. The fog clears. The next step becomes visible. And so begins your return to clarity. Her debut is an inspiring and transformative guide to personal development. She masterfully blends personal anecdotes with actionable insights, emphasizing the critical role of clarity in achieving self-awareness, setting meaningful goals, and living intentionally. Each chapter provides practical tools and strategies for navigating life's complexities with precision and purpose. 'Clarity Call' caters to individuals from all walks of life, making it a must-read for personal and professional growth."*

**— Earl Waud,**
**Bestselling author of Hindsight & Borrowed Belief, Coauthor of Unlocking Success with Jack Canfield, and Creator of AI Prompts for Profit Accelerator**

*"I went through Ami Rasheed's book 'Clarity Call' and found it as a work for transformative leadership. The book provides practical lessons for individuals, who seek personal growth and intentional living, with exercises and questions to reflect on. Ami's clear and engaging writing style makes complex concepts accessible to all, from children to professionals to achieve their fullest potential and lead a purposeful life."*

**—Zainudheen PB,**
**Group Executive Director of Hotpack,**
**UAE-based global food packaging manufacturer**

*"In a world of constant noise and distraction, Ami Rasheed's 'Clarity Call' is a beacon of light. This powerful guide reignited my sense of purpose. Ami doesn't just inspire—she equips you with practical tools to turn vision into reality. If you're feeling stuck or overwhelmed, this book is the clarity compass you've been searching for. A must-read for anyone ready to move from drifting to thriving."*

**— Muneer Amayoor,**
**Amazon bestselling author, trainer,**
**radio presenter & master Hypnotherapist**

*"It's a treasure for anyone who wants to gain a better understanding of themselves and then use the knowledge to transform their lives."*

**—Mamta Joshi,**
**Poet, Student Empowerment Coach**

*"This book is an absolute go-to for those who want to achieve their dreams but aren't sure how to go about it. The author has so much clarity on what she wants to offer her readers, and that reflects beautifully throughout the book. Clarity in itself. It provides a step-by-step guide on how to gain clarity and how that clarity can help in achieving one's goals. What I truly appreciate is the practical steps and relatable examples shared along the way."*

**—Safa Majeed,**
**CEO& Founder, Cvox360**

*"Ami Rasheed is such an empowered leader who desired to help those who may be stuck in confusion and lacking in confidence to face the future. Through her coaching, she introduces the practical steps towards one's desired goal. This book will be useful to boost confidence and excitement in your journey. Most importantly, it all begins with clarity in purpose and strategy."*

**—Nenette Santos,**
**Cognitive Behavioral Life Coach**

*"I found 'Clarity Call' by Ami Rasheed to be a priceless guide. The book's practical exercises and real-life examples make strategies for personal growth accessible. Its focus on self-discovery, goal setting, and aligning beliefs with values offers clear direction for anyone seeking fulfillment and improvement."*

**—Anish Mohan,**
**Productivity & Empowerment Coach**

# YOUR JOURNEY TO BECOMING A 'PERSON OF CLARITY'

**Clarity Checklist**

This checklist will help you evaluate your progress on your clarity journey. Focus and self-reflection will be your companions, while a cluttered mind and distractions will be your biggest enemies. Stay committed to decluttering your physical and mental space to unlock your highest potential.

**Daily Practices for Clarity:**

☑ Start with silence: Dedicate at least 30 minutes each day to sit with yourself in stillness. Let go of distractions and unclear thoughts. Do encourage stillness often.

☑ Find the best time for reflection: Identify when you are most receptive to deep thinking and self-awareness. Morning? Evening? Choose a time that works for you.

☑ Seek clarity by asking powerful, self-reflective questions.

☑ Reflect on your thoughts: Observe your thinking patterns. Write down any sparks of inspiration, stress triggers, fears, or recurring thoughts in your journal. Let us name it the 'Clarity Journal.' ' 'CJ'

☑ Watch your self-talk: Be mindful of your inner dialogue. If you catch yourself doubting, reframe it with positive clarity-based thinking.

☑ Keep it reachable: Always keep a journal with you to write down creative ideas and thoughts. (whether empowering or disempowering), triggers, emotions, and more.

☑ Find your purpose on this planet: You will learn how to identify it from the book. Your purpose is waiting for you.

☑ Live with intentionality: Every action, decision, and thought should align with your vision. Live with awareness, clarity, and purpose.

☑ Keep a peaceful mindset: Maintain a calm and stress-free mood throughout the day. Whenever negativity arises, pause, breathe, and reset your thoughts. You can!

☑ Read aloud your affirmations: Speak words of clarity, focus, and self-belief daily. Example: "My mind is clear and focused."

**Visualization & Goal-Setting**

☑ Read your vision and goals every morning and night: Keep them at the forefront of your mind by reviewing them daily. Place your written goals somewhere you can see them often.

☑ Look at your vision board: Spend time each day visualizing the life you are creating. See yourself achieving your dreams with clarity.

☑ Track your progress: Regularly cross-check completed goals and acknowledge your growth.

☑ Get an accountability partner: If you are a self-motivated person all the time, you can skip this part. If you need a push, get a best buddy to check on you, specifically regarding your goals.

Remember, the buddy is for accountability—no silly talks, no bragging.

☑ Create a mastermind group: Discuss your challenges with like-minded individuals. Be ready to sit in the hot seat and be challenged until you get things done.

☑ Read and revist key chapters: Reread the sections of this book that resonate with you. Find solutions for the challenges discussed in the book. The golden concept of 'clarity' will make you a highly successful leader by helping you forge a clear path. Here, you will discover who you are, who you want to be, what you want to have, and what you want to do with your life.

☑ Embrace clarity as a lifestyle: This book will help you understand why clarity plays a major role in living the life you want and enjoying the lifestyle you desire.

☑ Stay committed to your clarity journey, and watch as your vision unfolds with purpose and precision.

# PART I

# THE HOLY GRAIL OF CLARITY

*"Clarity is about who you are, where you are going, and how to get there"*

**– Brian Tracy,**
**Best-selling author and**
**Personal development expert**

# I) A JOURNEY FROM CONFUSION TO CLARITY

In the serene village beneath the Pandallur Hills in the South Indian state of Kerala, where whispers of history mingled with the simplicity of agrarian life, my dream of becoming a doctor shone brightly. Yet, my journey was fraught with obstacles, primarily due to a lack of clarity and proper guidance.

As I completed my twelfth grade, I was excited to start my journey toward my dream goal. Medicine was the only goal I had. However, uncertainty engulfed me like a dense fog, obscuring my path. I had no plan B. I couldn't achieve my dream due to some factors. Out of them was due to societal pressures as society expected girls to be wives and homemakers, not doctors, engineers, or pilots. Education was not a liberty they had.

Girls were married off after their 10th or 12th grade. In such a society, spending five years to become a doctor seemed not that valuable.

Another factor that prevented me from entering the medical field was a lack of clarity on how to get there, and whom to approach. The advice we got from the elders, was "Invest in Gold, not in education for girls".

To reach there, my dad had to sell his property, and he got advice that he could do that for my marriage. My dad got confused, and I was left with no clarity about my future.

He is an ex-expat, with an early retirement in his early forties for his great mission, to serve his mom. Because the day before he was planning to leave for the Middle East, my grand mom, tripped on the floor and got injured. He decided to serve her, rather than going back to the Middle East, to rejoin his job after his three-month vacation.

Despite my father's unwavering support, he was bound by the same norms that dictated a girl's future should align with traditional roles. I was now left with two choices; marriage, or a degree in something I had no interest in. I was totally against the idea of getting married back then, so to escape that I decided to pursue my Bachelor's Degree in Economics even though I had no interest in it as my passion was science. Thus, rather than following my passion, I was driven by confusion, stress, and fear.

### The Direction

My mentor's words came to my mind, "If you don't know where to take your life, others will decide your path based on their reality and experience. Without clarity, you will lose your destination."

I lacked direction, I chose economics to avoid letting others decide my future, as it was the lowest-hanging fruit I could opt for. I refused to let societal biases dictate my path.

Due to a lack of clarity in having a plan about what to do if not studying medicine. By the time I decided on a degree, all the admissions had closed.

I had to enroll in a private college. Still, my passion for science made me decide to pursue microbiology the next year when the new academic year started in the public colleges.

Once I started applying for microbiology after one year, my parents asked, what was wrong with a degree in economics. "No need to waste one year. You can lead a better life and raise your kids in the future, other than any of your relatives or friends, because you have a degree at least."

I gave more value to what people around me thought or said than my passion. Back then, I did not know how to find my passion or how to work for it. The advice I sought from doctors, teachers, and engineers was based on their own limited experiences, leaving me adrift in a sea of confusion.

### Invisible Counselors

I didn't understand the importance of having the right mentor to guide me, even though I wished for someone to help. I was wishing for an invisible person to guide me.

However, no invisible person came, and no magic wand helped me. I didn't know the Jose Silva method of visualization, to call up on my invisible counselors then. I had to go with my intuition, which I didn't do.

I couldn't find the right person at the time, which led to me discarding my dreams. Even though I graduated with good marks, the certificate did not bring me happiness. I felt like it did not belong to me.

### Social Conditioning

In a community where marriage was considered a priority for a girl, the pressure to get married increased as I completed my Bachelor's. My new aim was to find a Master's course to escape marriage. I didn't want a master's in Economics.

Eventually, I decided to pursue a postgraduate in fields like business, journalism, or humanities, however, the right path seemed hard to find.

I eventually pursued a Master's in English Language and Literature, driven by an intense desire to learn.

## My Battle with English Language skills

Here too, I faced many challenges, especially with English literature and phonetics, which were completely new to me.

"Awareness and acceptance of reality are the first steps towards transforming challenges". I had to stretch myself a lot to learn the basics of the English language and literature. I realized that I couldn't understand anything.

On the very first day of my class, our Head of the Department (HoD) asked me to speak in English on the college premises, however, I couldn't say anything other than my name, having studied in my regional language until 10th grade.

In my class, there were only seven students, including three girls and four boys. Two of the girls were married and had children, and the boys were working part-time.

On the days when I was alone in the classroom, I would be shy looking at the faces of male professors. I fidgeted with my hands and legs, during the classes, without knowing how to spend the whole period. I was referred to as the class representative by everyone. In most cases, I became a laughingstock in the class.

Whenever my classmates discussed what they had learned in their graduation, I remained silent. I couldn't understand anything when they talked about 19th and 20th-century literature. My desire to learn the basics of English language and literature led me to take an oath to myself.

## My Leap Towards Learning

I decided that every weekend, I would visit the best university library, which was the only one I could access within my limited means.

I traveled over 50 kilometers to learn the basics of English literature, accompanied by my supportive father or alone, driven by my thirst for knowledge. Finally, though my academic success brought high scores which did not satisfy me or my dreams.

Without a clear path, I drifted into a teacher's training program, with two options which were only available in Bangalore, India, then.

## Dreams have no Boundaries

Dreaming of establishing an educational institution for underprivileged girls, made me unstoppable. My ambitions stretched beyond societal expectations, and I applied for a passport, hoping to explore opportunities abroad. During my teacher's training program in Bangalore, I tasted a newfound freedom, free from the constant pressure of marriage brokers. For a few months, I worked in some schools and for a reputed bank in Bangalore, determined not to return to my village immediately.

## My Experiment with Failures

However, differing opinions with my parents eventually brought me back home. The challenges of a commission-based sales job in the bank were disheartening, and my father's concern for my well-being prompted my return to the village.

I couldn't understand the basics of sales and failed miserably in front of every customer. Every morning, our manager would brief us on what we had to do for the day, our targets, how to build our franchise, how to get promotions, and how to greet customers. All those teachings went over my head. At the end of the session, we had a game where we had to keep some amount of money, and the team would stand in a circle. The money would be circulated among the team, and my teammates would win while I was left scratching my head, by figuring out how they were winning.

Amidst my teacher training, my marriage was arranged. After returning from Bangalore, we got married. He was a Dubai-based journalist, Rasheed Palliyalil. He is now a Public Relations expert embarking on a new chapter of my life in Dubai, UAE.

## Be an Eternal Student

I still hadn't stopped my studies, and this person supported me throughout my journey. It has been 16 years now, we are leading a purposeful living with our two brilliant kids, in the city of Dubai, enjoying all the freedom, and learning, leading, and growing happily.

## Mentors are Lighthouses

From this unclear journey of pursuing many streams, the message I discovered is this: first, envision where you see yourself in six or seven years, the lifestyle you want, the kind of office you work in, and the possessions you aspire to have. Before you take action on your dream, seek help from experts until you are satisfied. Do not compromise with the available people or the so-called educated people. They would not be able to help you, where experts can! Which I did.

Secondly, your association plays a major role in your personal growth. The people whom you are surrounded with would influence your life.

This lesson profoundly influenced my journey, guiding me toward the path I eventually followed. My story is a testament to the power of clarity and the importance of seeking proper guidance to illuminate the path to one's true calling. Once I learned the concept of clarity, I wished, I had known this back then.

# II) FINDING MY VOICE DURING THE PANDEMIC

During the initial months of the outbreak of the COVID-19 pandemic in 2020, the city of Dubai witnessed cop cars patrolling around the streets to alert the residents and announce, "Stay safe at home for your loved ones, your safety is our priority."

My family and I looked outside at the cop vehicles and listened to the alert message from the balcony of our modest apartment in the city's busy residential area, which turned empty in those days.

### Leadership Responsibility

Living in a metropolis city like Dubai, I could reflect on this message from a leadership dimension. What is it? Visionary leaders demonstrate responsibility through effective crisis communication, uniting people and fostering collective action. Their proactive measures reinforce resilience and a shared sense of duty. With a clear vision and mission, they ensure society remains strong, united, and prepared for the future.

The pandemic altered our lives in various ways and forms. Hundreds of job losses, separation from loved ones, and the spread of the infection were common experiences, often leading to severe trauma and stress.

However, amidst the struggles, some individuals and organizations discovered opportunities for growth by changing strategies. They found new options to beat the situation. Those who embraced new strategies, adapted to changing systems, and stayed flexible ultimately achieved remarkable success, and even became millionaires.

## Connecting Minds: The Surge of E-learning

During the pandemic, online study options boomed with platforms like Zoom and Microsoft Teams. Additionally, there were numerous free webinars available, enhancing people's opportunities for learning and skill development from the comfort of their homes.

People started to learn more about these platforms. I also started attending online classes and embraced technology. I always loved to be an eternal student. Learning has been a continuous journey for me.

However, I didn't know the importance of vertical learning. I realized I was growing horizontally. What did this mean? I was learning multiple things and different subjects like the Neuro Linguistic Program (NLP), personality development, gardening, relationship theory, and so forth.

During this time, I attended an online boot camp titled 'Speak and Spark' by Farookh Sensei, who had turned from international martial arts champion to an instructor of pilots to a leadership master coach.

The boot camp focused on professional speaking and presentation practice with in-depth knowledge, practical tips, and a system for professional speaking, especially to master in conducting online sessions or setting up online universities.

I loved Sensei's 'power voice', enthusiasm, and charismatic personality. He taught his students the importance of emptying their cups, before learning new things. That means we must be able to receive wisdom without any judgement.

During the session, he surprised us by revealing that he had presented nearly 400 PowerPoint slides in that hour-long session. In the end, he asked for feedback via WhatsApp, promising a gift for selected messages.

After sending my feedback, I received a reply offering a soft copy of his then-latest book and some video teachings about leadership.

I decided to consider him as my mentor, during the session itself. It was a 'Hurray' moment. I felt like I found my mentor. I just wanted to be his student and learn from him, leadership wisdom and presentation skills. As he mentioned during the session, I needed to learn vertically, not horizontally, in order to reach my desired destination.

### The Discovery Call

I approached him to join his session. For more clarity and understanding of myself, at first, I sat for a discovery coaching session with him, during which he asked, "What is the one thing you want to accomplish in the next two to five years?"

The very first question left me tongue-tied. I could sense a cold silence. It was a complete 360-degree shift in my thought, perspective and learning. This 90-minute discovery session jolted me awake. For the first time, I understood the real cost of playing small. Without designing my days and taking bold, consistent action, my dream would remain just that, a dream.

Sensei asked a powerful question.

"Imagine you've achieved your dream. What does it smell like? How does it feel? What color surrounds it? What sounds echo around you? Who's there, appreciating you?"

I wanted to leap from my chair, filled with emotion, yet I stayed silent, too shy to put the feeling into words. He continued,

You know where you want to be. However, dreams require sharpened skills and daily effort. So, what's the one thing you'll do right after this session to create massive impact?

That question didn't leave me. It followed me into the night. I couldn't sleep. My mind raced with ideas, a stirring realization that I had so much to offer the world. That's when I knew transformation starts with silence, reflection, and purposeful movement.

As the session wrapped up, he asked me to spell the word "Excuse."

"E-X-C-U-S-E," I replied.

"If there are no excuses, I can push you forward. And when you're ready, I won't let you sour low. I will make sure you soar high."

That line stayed with me. It felt like a personal promise.

Later, I learned he had authored several books, and my close friend had edited his then-latest one. That connection lit spark in me. I quietly visualized myself as his next editor, and years later, that vision came true. Possibilities expanded.

Before closing the call, he gave me a final assignment:

Bring five dream roles or businesses you have in mind. Then narrow it to two and finally, choose one.

That moment hit hard. It demanded clarity. It stripped away the noise. And for the first time, my dream had a direction. It wasn't just about dreaming big, it was about choosing where to begin.

## My Leadership Lessons and Realizations

I started **pondering** and reflecting on 'who I am', and why should I exist on this planet. I searched for my passion. I started to find out what kind of personality I was, and a lot more questions about myself. Everything happens for a reason, right? That was the right time to pursue my dream.

I once believed that I would achieve my dream one day. Later, I've realized that "one day" is always out of reach. Real change happens through small, intentional actions, repeated consistently over time, building momentum and leading to transformation.

I **discovered** the importance of having crystal clear clarity on where I am taking my life, and what am I doing right now.

I **discovered** the importance of having a clear goal by setting a time frame and strategies to achieve it. Sensei always reminded me that consistency is the key to being successful.

I **learned** that I need to raise my standards to become valuable for myself and valuable for others. No school ever taught me these life gems.

I **realized** that my postgraduate education and various learning programs meant nothing unless I moved forward from where I was. Degrees are just papers if I don't apply my knowledge to my professional or personal growth. My qualifications didn't serve me as I had hoped because I lacked clarity about my passion and vision. I also hadn't understood the difference between passion and interest, before, I was merely interested and found excuses to stay in my shell. My competency was not up to the mark when it came to chasing my dreams.

Earlier, I was so eager to change the world, however, I refused to change myself intentionally, and I was not ready to stretch. I used to keep my learnings and leadership within my comfort zone.

My comfort zone shattered, pushing me to share my knowledge and step into a new horizon. Shifting from learning for myself to learning for impact transformed my approach to leadership and action.

I **learned** that leadership starts from our homes itself. I asked myself, why do I need to teach the importance of leadership to my kids at a young age and how can I teach them to be influential? This helped me understand the power of self-reflective questions.

I **reflected** on the importance of having the right support, whether it's a coach, a mentor, a strong community, or an accountability buddy to help me push through challenges.

**Here are a Few Self-reflective Questions that I asked Myself:**

What is the next bold step to lead myself and lead others like great leaders?

What footprint should I leave behind? What is the one unique solution I can offer to the world?

What am I doing right now to serve my people?

What have I been doing in my life until now? This question made me understand the importance of the 'value of time.'

What are the things I need to change immediately to take the first step?

What are my strengths to start something new?

What is the one area that I can focus on, to start with?

Why do I need to start acting on my mission now?

What obstacles have overshadowed my ability to manifest my desires?

I gained clarity on my journey to greatness, envisioning paths to my grandest vision and manifesting my dreams daily. With him, I embarked on this journey. The pandemic deepened my perspective on clarity and growth.

From there onwards I call clarity **'diamond-cut clarity'** because it means making something very clear and easy to understand, just like how a diamond is cut to make it sparkle and shine.

Clarity, like a diamond, is formed through intense pressure and refinement. Just as a diamond transforms from a raw carbon to a brilliant gem through precise cutting and polishing, clarity emerges when you consciously refine your thoughts, eliminate distractions, and align with your true purpose. The thoughts about diamond-cut clarity made me earn more pieces of wisdom and become more resourceful in life.

### Chat with Champion

The realization of having a coach came to me after meeting Manoj Vasudevan, the Singapore-based Toastmasters World Champion of Public Speaking, in 2017, which led me to pursue one. He is a Next Level Leadership Readiness Coach, author and founder of Thought Expressions, a management consultancy. Details of this encounter and the profound impact it had on my decision to seek a coach will be narrated in a subsequent chapter.

Learning from all the mistakes in my life, I understood that without clarity, I lost my sense of direction. I ended up studying different streams due to a lack of clarity and mentors in my life. I struggled a lot through that journey. I understood that I could leverage my time if I associated with the best of the best people in my life.

I wrote this book after understanding the importance of clarity in my life. I understood that the price of clarity in one's life is huge, and it should be there, since childhood, especially during one's school and college days.

Because of clarity and finding my purpose, I got many opportunities, including interviews with great leaders like the World Champion of Public Speaking and other experts. I stood alongside the world champion to address a large audience in the UAE, to talk about my project and many more leading programs in the UAE.

Someone taught me the importance of clarity and adding value to others' lives. Now it is my duty and responsibility to bring clarity to others' lives so that they can also grow beyond their wildest dreams and goals. They can be a part of my mission in life. My purpose is to guide me in helping others stay aligned with their mission.

Now let me do my responsibility to teach others what I have learned from my experience. You will get all the information you need to gain clarity on what you set for yourself. Don't just read! I guarantee you success if you reflect and write answers to those questions in your 'CJ'.

You will discover that by following strategies and designing your days starting reflection, you too can grow beyond your limits, and lead a happy and content life. I will show you how to work on your dreams by creating a movie-like picture within yourself of diamond-cut clarity and certainty.

Congratulations on taking the first step to read, 'Make the Clarity Call to Yourself' and seeking clarity for your life journey! It's evident that you want to improve and grow in areas like health, wealth, self-development, relationships, and spirituality. Trust in your potential. To achieve clarity and discover your blind spots, sit beside you with compassion and listen to what your soul says. Judgements, and limiting beliefs are out. This will guide you on a powerful inner journey, one that helps you uncover your true identity, reconnect with your purpose, and awaken the next version of who you're meant to become.

Start small, and avoid relying on luck. It will be helpful if you dedicate 20 minutes daily over the next 90 days to read and journal your thoughts about your journey, setting yourself on the path to chasing your dreams.

I encourage you to get ready with your 'CJ' and practice. I wish you all the best.

# CHAPTER 1

# CLARITY BLUEPRINT

*"Clarity of vision is the key to achieving your objectives."*

**– Tom Steyer,**

**American investor and businessman**

Imagine you're on the verge of completing the biggest dream project of your life. You've poured in months of dedication, carefully crafted strategies, and put unwavering commitment. Success is within reach. However, in a single, shocking moment, everything falls apart. Your project, design, your masterpiece, vanishes from your computer, like a bolt of lightning. Suddenly, you're left staring at a blank screen, your heart racing.

It feels like the ground has crumbled beneath you, pulling you into a downward spiral of panic and disbelief.

In that moment, you're consumed by fear. Will you lose the project? Your job? Your confidence evaporates, and uncertainty takes over. Your mind races and no clear solution emerges. You're stuck, paralyzed by doubt and overwhelmed by the sheer weight of it all.

This is what it feels like to lose clarity. Here you can't see the path ahead. Something like foggy. Even if it's just for a half an hour or a few minutes, that loss of focus and direction can feel devastating. The fog of uncertainty blinds you, making every step feel impossible.

What if, in that moment of chaos, you could tap into a sense of calm, purpose, and clear direction? What if you could shift from panic to patience and attain liberation from fear?

In the '*Clarity Call*', you're going to learn exactly how to do that. You're going to discover the transformative power of clarity, how it can guide you through life's most uncertain moments and unlock a deep well of confidence and productivity.

Clarity isn't just a luxury. It's the key to achieving your greatest ambitions, even when the world seems to be falling apart. It is essential for everyone, regardless of background.

Let me explain this concept with a story. It was a sunny afternoon. The house was quiet, with only the sound of birds chirping outside.

Nina, a curious girl of ten, was visiting her grandmother's old house. She liked exploring the attic, it smelled of old books and stories waiting to be found. It felt special like it had a story to tell. As she looked around, her eyes fell on a dusty wooden box tucked in a corner. Curious, she picked it up and opened it slowly. To her surprise, inside was a shining diamond. It sparkled even in the dim light, resting quietly among old ribbons and papers.

Through Nina's story and beyond, we'll explore how clarity is often a process of rediscovery, revealing who you are and the direction you want to take. As you delve deeper into this chapter, think of clarity as the diamond in your own attic, something already within you, waiting to be uncovered and polished, guiding you toward the life you truly desire.

Nina brought the diamond to her grandmother, her eyes wide with excitement.

Her grandmother looked at it, then at Nina, and smiled softly.

"I thought I'd lost this forever," she said, taking the diamond in her wrinkled hands. "Your grandfather gave it to me a long time ago. It was very special."

She dusted it gently with a soft cloth and placed it near the window where the sunlight was falling in a narrow stream.

"Let me show you something magical," she whispered.

As the light passed through the diamond, something beautiful happened. The plain white beam broke into a splash of colors, violets, reds, greens, and blues, that danced across the walls like little fairies.

Nina gasped. "It's like a rainbow!"

Her grandmother chuckled. "Yes, light hides many colors. However, the diamond helps us see them."

Nina's eyes sparkled brighter than the diamond itself. She sat beside her grandmother, asking all sorts of questions, about light, rainbows, and the magic hidden in simple things.

And in that moment, surrounded by the soft colors on the walls and her grandmother's stories, Nina knew she had found something more than just a treasure. She had found wonder.

She started asking so many questions, like why do the colors move when I move the diamond? Does the sun always have these colors inside it? Can I make this happen with other things too? Is white light really made of all these colors? How can a diamond do that?

When she asks questions, she reflects. It helps her uncover hidden assumptions, clear confusion, challenge limiting beliefs and lead to more informed decisions. Doubt made her pause, reflect, and discover what she truly wanted and believed.

> ***"Asking questions is the starting point of clarity.***

Her grandmother explained it in detail, by saying that when I was a young girl, like you, I had also watched this kind of process with curiosity. And she added each color is special, like our lives, adding to a picture of endless possibilities.

Her grandmother added, "This diamond is your state of clarity. When it's clear, it can transform simple light into a spectrum of beautiful possibilities." As the colors swirled and intertwined, Nina's grandmother continued, the different colors represent endless possibilities.

Just as the diamond reveals the hidden richness of light, clarity in your lives can unveil the vast spectrum of opportunities and choices waiting to be embraced. Life is all about choice. It could be good or bad. It is up to you what you choose.

Her grandmother added, "Adjusting the angle of the diamond alters the light, just like adjusting your mindset with clear thoughts brings clarity". It's like reprogramming your brain from time to time. She added taking care of your mind is your responsibility, as all of your activities and thoughts are governed by this powerful organ.

Clarity is your mind's nature. Allow your mind to clear by itself. Just as the diamond needs sunlight to show its colors, your minds need clear thoughts to reveal the endless opportunities in life.

Nina felt the diamond was telling her a story, one filled with colors, wonder, and a journey waiting to begin.

Look at the image given below. Just as sunlight, when focused, reveals a hidden rainbow through a crystal, when channeled through clarity, unfolds the full spectrum of your inner gifts. Clarity doesn't add anything new; it simply helps us see what was always there, waiting to shine. But for clarity to truly reflect its brilliance, it needs space, space to breathe, and thoughts that are calm, focused, and aligned."

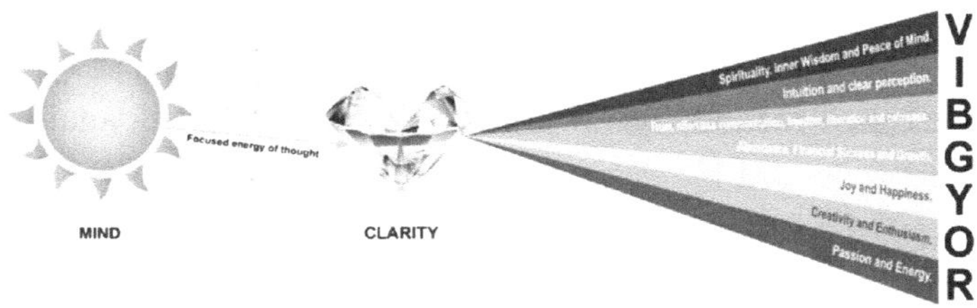


Her grandmother asked her to apply this technique to her life, to win big. With this newfound insight, she approached her own life with a sense of purpose, direction and clarity, especially in her studies. Every choice she made was like a brushstroke, adding bright colors to the picture of her life.

She felt her thoughts must be as bright as the sun's rays or diamonds. Both are clear in nature. She understood that she needed to dust it often, so that she could score good marks in her school, and maintain a healthy relationship with her parents, teachers and friends so that she could enjoy a peaceful life. She started setting her goals high!

Like a dusty diamond, when you expose it to the sunlight after cleaning, your mind can find clarity, regardless of past or present circumstances, when you introspect, aware, and sometimes with a bit of patience. It doesn't matter how cluttered your mind may be; with the right mindset, you can brush off the dust just as Nina did with the diamond. Fresh thoughts, ideas, and possibilities await. Clarity holds the solution to overcoming any challenges you may face.

## Unblocking Clarity

As Nina discovered, clarity waits behind the scenes. It appears when she prepares her mind. With self-reflection, she creates a pathway for it to emerge.

She asked herself, "What if I held a wooden block against the sunlight? It would block the light. Similarly, if my mind is filled with unwanted thoughts, every opportunity may be blocked for me. So, I will protect my mind by clearing away negative thoughts, allowing happiness to flow freely. In this sense", clarity is pure joy, pure freedom.

## Clarity Emerges within

Let us talk more about clarity. It doesn't matter who you are, or what background you come from. If you don't have clarity, you get stuck in your life. If you don't have clarity, you can't reach where you want to reach, and you can't become who you want to be, regardless of how much experience you have because you feel uncertain or confused about your desires and priorities, making it difficult to make decisions or take purposeful actions toward your desired outcomes. Everything is cluttered or unclear.

"Clarity precedes success," said Robin Sharma, author and leadership expert, in his book "Megaliving".

Without clarity, you might wander aimlessly like a leaf in the wind. The wind controls the leaf's movement. Here, the wind represents distractions, which are the enemies of clarity.

> ***"To take your life to the destination and navigate beyond it, you need to understand the law of the brain. It is nothing but clarity".***

With clarity, you know, what to do with your life. You will find ways to find your 'how' and 'where you are taking' your life. You know the pace of your work. You know why you are going in that direction. You know the challenges in front of you. You know the skills you need to improve or work on. You know how to say 'No' to 99 things to stay laser-focused, even though those 99 ideas are creative. You know how to have peace with yourself, then to be at peace with your environment.

I strongly agree with Brian Tracy's thought, which we mentioned in the introduction of this book.

Imagine yourself as the experienced captain of your life, equipped with the expertise to navigate every twist and turn of the journey. Even among the most turbulent times, you, as the expert captain, skillfully find a new path to reach your destination as planned.

Clarity is crucial. When you have clarity, your mind is "in order." It stays focused on the task at hand, free from confusion. Confusion drains your energy and time. It's essential to be clear about your specific task.

Before joining the leadership program led by Sensei, I associated the term "clarity" primarily with optics, such as the clarity of a torch, light, spectrum, or lens, or clarity of a well-lit path, and clarity in communication.

Little did I know about the profound impact of clarity on personal development then. Clarity, as it turns out, is a powerful force in one's journey.

If you possess clarity about your vision, goal, purpose, passion, strengths, weaknesses, values, beliefs, thought patterns, mindset, and communication you become unstoppable. Clarity becomes your superpower.

## The State of Clarity

Imagine what would be the result, if you had a clear head, if you could see your life as if you were watching a beautiful movie, whenever you feel?

The author of 'The Little Book of Clarity', Jamie Smart, starts his book with the following words:

"If a pond is clouded with mud, there is nothing you can do to make the water clear. But when you allow the mud to settle, it will clear on its own, because clarity is the water's natural state."

He added that clarity is the brain's natural state. It means just as a pond becomes clear when the mud settles, the mind achieves clarity when disturbances and distractions are allowed to settle. This suggests that clarity is the mind's natural state, as Jamie Smart opined and by allowing thoughts to settle, one can achieve a clear and focused mind. This is the idea of dusting off the diamond as well.

It emphasizes the importance of patience and calmness in achieving mental clarity, rather than forcing the process to happen.

It's you who creates clutter in your mind with unfiltered thoughts. To achieve clarity, you need a sieve to filter those thoughts. Just as you apply filters to your videos to enhance their appeal, you must be mindful of the filters you use in your mind. Your brain is your precious gift, yet the brain often become clouded with unwanted thoughts that hinder your progress.

Clarity is pure and genuine. It is the embodiment of truth. With a clear mind, everything becomes as transparent as water. You understand how to set goals precisely and achieve them.

Simultaneously, if you are stressed or frustrated, bring your mind to a state of clarity. The reality is that every person has a source of knowledge and insight within them. What you need is some quality time to reflect, pause for a while, ponder, and write it down. Listen to your intuition.

## The Illuminators

There is always a great possibility that you can seek help from a coach, mentor, or specialist when you get stuck. What does a coach do there? Nothing but helping you to reach your insight level.

The coach helps clear away the clutter in your mind, creating a calm and relaxed state for reflection. The coach holds the torch, guiding the way, however, the light comes from within you. Coaching helps you discover and connect with your own inner light to move forward. Then, you gain the insight needed to move forward.

I never believed this until I experienced a clarity coaching session by myself. Previously, I often relied on both my circle of friends and acquaintances, irrespective of their expertise in the same field or experience, and sought guidance from experts in various fields to navigate each step. Once I completed my coaching session with Sensei, I learned that I need a coach or mentor to get clarity, and I understood that I am the sole clarifier and the coach is the illuminator. The outcome was truly magical.

## Clarity as the GPS

Clarity is very important in your professional and personal life. It is a state of mind in which you are more focused, and your perception is clear. With mental clarity, you can recognize, understand, and organize your thoughts, like Nina, does. Clarity is a state in which your mind is fully active and engaged, and more over-focused on one single dot at a time.

You and I need clarity to work through our daily tasks and stay productive throughout the day. If you have clarity, you can see things clearly as day, so you are helping your mind reduce the task, by pre-planning your day.

See your future as clear as a bright sunny day. See that future destination and future self, as if you are playing that video in your mind. You must be ready to adjust your destination, throughout the journey, only then you will reach your destination.

Sensei compared clarity with the GPS, explaining that just like you can adjust your GPS when you veer off course, you can guide your mind by setting a clear destination. Even if you take detours, the GPS will provide directions to get you back on track. It will say, "Turn left, turn right, make a U-turn," and so on until you reach your destination safely.

Similarly, you must give your brain a clear destination, before you set your course, as it works in pictures. To reach your desired destination, you need to send the right message to your brain. You need to maintain clarity until your last breath.

### Call to Action

Have you made your clarity call today?

What empowering questions are rising within you after reading this chapter? Take a moment to sit with them.

CHAPTER 2

# CLARITY: A CATALYST FOR HIGH PERFORMANCE

*"The successful warrior is the average man, with laser-like focus."*

**– Bruce Lee,**
**Legendary martial arts guru and philosopher**

In this chapter, let us look into the linguistic and etymological roots of clarity. Clarity is defined as the quality of being coherent and intelligible. Another definition of clarity is the quality of transparency and purity.

Now let us look at the etymology of clarity. The word 'clarity' comes from the Latin term 'Claritas', which means 'clearness' or 'brightness'.

It is derived from the adjective 'clarus,' meaning 'clear' or 'bright'. The term evolved through Old French 'clarité' before entering the English language in the late Middle Ages.

Over time, "clarity" has come to signify not only physical clearness but also mental and intellectual transparency, emphasizing the quality of being easily understood or free from ambiguity.

## Understanding the Superpower

*"Knowing your purpose allows concentration"*

**– Peter Drucker, Austrian-American consultant and educator.**

Clarity is the quality of being clear and easy to understand, like when you can see through a window so well that you don't even notice it's there. It is also like water that is crystal clear or having a clean lens that helps you focus on what matters the most.

Clarity is the ability to see things as they truly are, without confusion or distractions. Understanding the importance of clarity is like discovering a superpower for your growth. You can say that it's about clearing the mental fog so you can move forward with purpose and direction.

It empowers you to live authentically, make choices aligned with your true selves, and appreciate the beauty that surrounds you. So, let us embrace the transformative power of clarity.

> **"*Clarity is about clearing roadblocks and obstacles one by one through regular reflection. It isn't a fixed state, it's an ongoing journey. It has no final destination.***

# THE DIFFERENCE BETWEEN A PERSON WITH CLARITY AND A PERSON WHO FEELS STUCK

A person with clarity has a clear understanding of goals, vision, purpose, values, and direction, whereas a person who feels stuck, lacks goals, vision, values, and direction.

A person with clarity is laser-focused, knowing how to prioritize their most important tasks, whereas a person who lacks clarity gets easily distracted. A person with clarity has great confidence because their thoughts are organized, whereas a person who lacks clarity experiences self-doubt and lacks confidence.

A person with clarity has control over his thoughts and feelings, scanning them effectively, whereas the other person has no control over their thoughts and feelings due to tension and worry.

A person with clarity creates a roadmap, making them unstoppable, whereas the other person goes with the flow and gets lost along the way. A person with clarity reflects and adjusts their roadmap, whereas the other person follows a monotonous cycle.

> ***Clear minds spark quick actions, concise words, and unwavering purpose. People with clear minds, attract positive whispers and deflect the echoes of negativity.***

A person with clarity creates continuous progress, with consistency being their key, whereas a person who lacks clarity sees no progress. A person with clarity loves to live in the moment and can live happily, whereas a person who lacks clarity always worries about the past and future, lacking peace of mind. A person with clarity adapts to changes and brings creativity to whatever they do, whereas a person who lacks clarity resists change, leading to a lack of creativity.

## The Benefits of Clarity

In both personal and professional contexts, clarity has many benefits. Clarity is like a magic key that unlocks success and joy. Clear thinking is the end product of clarity. It turns your vision into reality. It helps enhance productivity & satisfaction because you are sure of what you want to achieve, what you want to accomplish, what skillset and mindset you need to develop, and so forth.

With clarity, you know how to demonstrate the tasks to your team, because your mind is at peace. Your thoughts are well organised.

A person with a clear mind often rehearses his/her thoughts before speaking, even with family members. This practice ensures their words hit the mark and resonate with others. They have a clear idea about what not to say. With clarity you can make great decisions.

Clear communication fosters stronger connections, unlike the confusion caused by an unclear mind. By speaking directly and effectively, this person naturally connects better with people. You have clear thoughts, without any distractions. That builds your confidence, self-worth, and self-esteem. With that clarity, you have more authority than people without clarity.

When it comes to getting things done, you know how to prioritise your tasks, and set boundaries that avoid procrastination and thus enhance productivity.

A person with clarity loves himself or herself. You know how to appreciate yourself, and its benefits. You are good at appreciating your team's little wins, and through that, you can build your relationship and thus enjoy a better connection.

Clarity makes it easier for others to support you. A person of clarity is good at leadership, creativity, and adaptability.

Now you know the meaning of clarity, and how it serves us in any tough situations. Like the GPS, it directs you on your trip, and clarity drives you to your destination with laser focus by strong strategy and action. Distractions don't stand a chance against this powerful force.

## Call to Action

Let me share with you a story of mine, lacking clarity in communication, leading to an unfulfilled outcome. One weekend, I suggested going to a historical museum with my then 10-year-old daughter, Noura. She didn't like the idea. Without preparing how to communicate the idea, without explaining why it might be fun for her, she felt unheard and sad, refusing to cooperate and suggesting going to a shopping mall alone to buy things for each of the family members, their favorite things by herself.

I felt she was too small to go there alone, as the mentioned shopping mall was too big for her to locate different shops to buy different items for us. However, she has a clear idea of how to manage it.

Despite going to the mall, tension lingered, ruining the bonding experience. My message is that without clarity, you can't convincingly express your ideas, even to your kids, leading to stress, and disappointment, spoiling the weekend. You won't be able to persuade your kids or team too.

Now I want you to recall a situation where clarity played a vital role in communication or decision-making, leading to a positive outcome. It could be presenting in front of your clients your creativity. You can choose any of your stories.

Reflect on the happiness or satisfaction you felt in that moment. By doing this, you can appreciate the tangible impact of clarity in real-life scenarios.

# CHAPTER 3

# DECODING CLARITY

*"Leadership is more about clarity than it is about control."*

**– Mark Goulston, American psychiatrist, executive coach and consultant**

Imagine feeling lost and overwhelmed, like a traveler in a dense forest with no clear path forward. Let us take the example of Nina. Once she understood the concept of clarity, she could transform her confusion into a clear, focused vision. She learned to lead her life with intention, articulate her goals, and achieve remarkable results.

Let us join Nina on her journey as she decodes the essence of clarity and discovers how it can illuminate the path to success for anyone willing to embrace its principles.

## C for Clear or Coachable

It was only because Nina was coachable that she could make informed decisions about her future and studies. She embraced her grandmother's wisdom, reflected on it, and gained clarity. Coachability is the hallmark of a great leader.

With newfound clarity, she was able to create a clear roadmap and become laser-focused. Before achieving this clarity, she did one crucial thing: she dusted off the diamond, likewise, she cleared her mind, to make a strong decision. She listed out her goals based on priority.

### L for Leadership or Love Herself

Nina understood that to score higher marks in school, she needed to take the lead in her own life. She understood that first, she must be able to lead herself, then only she can lead others.

She became proactive, taking control of her decisions and actions. She established a timetable for both her studies and recreation, allowing herself to relax after reaching each milestone. She understood that to lead, she needed to design her days and create a blueprint for herself. She knew the importance of appreciating her little wins.

### A for Articulation/Action

The letter 'A' can be considered for amplification, action, achievement and articulation as well. You can choose the best-suited word for you, as your journey is your own. I choose the word 'articulation' to explain the letter 'A'.

Nina discovered that by setting clear goals and articulating her desires and results, it was easy for others to support her. She took massive action on her goals and achieved higher marks than before.

### R for Reality

Nina became fully aware of her reality, where she stood and who she was in that moment. Facing this reality allowed her to balance ambition with practicality.

She embraced her strengths while continuing to work on areas for growth. She didn't feel bad about her weaker subjects because, as a person of clarity, she understood that each student is different and unique. This understanding of reality only added more enthusiasm and commitment to her journey.

As Nina's self-awareness deepened, her learning became more effective. With unwavering commitment, she was able to achieve far more than she initially imagined.

## I for Intention

Nina knows intention is the fuel for clarity. She has clear reasons for why she does what she does. She sets positive intentions for her actions, ensuring they align with her values and beliefs.

Your beliefs impact every area of your life. Practice saying empowering beliefs to yourself like, "I am unstoppable when it comes to success, "I am loved", or "I can easily manifest my dreams", you may add more here based on your current reality. What specific actions will you take today, this week, or this month to continue your momentum?

## T for Tactic

Nina developed practical tactics to overcome obstacles. Tactics are her small milestones, like dividing time for each subject, time to do homework, and so forth. Her grandmother helped her to set her timetable.

She knew focusing on micro wins would give her a boost to move forward. She understood by celebrating small wins, she could bring more results and finally reach her macro goal, which is to become the topper in the school.

## Y for Yielding Result

Nina's efforts bore fruit. Through persistence and dedication, she began to achieve the results she had aimed for, making herself, her parents, and her school proud. A person with clarity can yield greater results than a confused mind ever could. Let us conclude this chapter with the help of the above acronym,

"Clarity is the result of leading life intentionally, by articulating goals clearly, and setting a world-class mindset, with eagle's focus to yield results. The outcome of clarity is a greater result".

## Call to Action

Have you set strong intentions to achieve your wildest dreams? What was the outcome you received? Were you happy with that?

CHAPTER 4

# THE PRINCIPLES OF CLARITY

Astronomer and mathematician Galileo Galilei once said,

> *"All truths are easy to understand once they are discovered. The point is to discover them. That takes investigation.*

I believe clarity is knowing the truth with direction. Here is my way to define clarity. Seeking truth through observation and experimentation.

Investigating yourselves requires a systematic and objective approach to self-awareness. It is quite simple. 'Clarity' is how children set the standard to find out the truth. How did they get amazed and become satisfied with the simple joys of life?

They are loving and open-hearted. They are curious to learn from the activities they fail in, getting up each time they fall until they succeed. The number of failures doesn't bother them. They focus on what they want. Not on circumstances. Not on people around them. Not on naysayers. Not on the weather. Not on the climate. Only on what they are committed to.

They connect easily with others with their innate ability to smile, with clarity. Have you ever seen them dwell on the past? Never, right? Unlike us, they live in the present.

Live in the present, without dwelling on the past, and be open to learning. Always be ready with an empty cup so that you can fill it with valuable wisdom, learning, and skill.

'Empty the cup' is a metaphor that means to let go of preconceived notions, biases, or past knowledge to make room for new ideas, learning, or insights. It suggests approaching situations with an open mind and a willingness to absorb fresh perspectives, without being clouded by previous experiences or judgments.

The phrase comes from a Zen story where a teacher demonstrates to students that they cannot learn new wisdom if their mind is already full, like a cup that cannot hold more water if it is already filled to the brim. To learn or grow, one must "empty the cup" first.

Sensei convinced me to love the concept of clarity. He taught me this concept in such a way that it is crystal clear in my mind, he taught at first through his one-on-one session and then through his group coaching.

I decided to help others too to love the concept of clarity. I consider bringing clarity to others' lives as a leadership responsibility. Because clarity is rewarding. It is the diamond people miss in life. It is the key to ultimate joy and prosperity.

Some years ago, I interviewed Manoj Vasudevan, Toastmasters World Champion of Public Speaking for a podcast. During the interview, he guided me with clarity about book writing.

He told me that people who want to write often have some initial limiting beliefs, like whether they have anything new to say, or whether people are going to buy their book, etc. You write a book that you like to read, so that even if nobody buys the book, at least you have a book to read. With that aspect, you will find similar others who would like to read your book. Target a certain group of people. If you do not know who the group is, choose yourself as the person, or write a book that you wish to read.

When you write about something you're passionate about, you invest 100% of your soul, body, and effort into it. As a result, the quality of the work will naturally shine, and there's no room for compromise.

From that conversation what I understood was that I needed to be clear about my passion, values, faith, and purpose aligned with. Of course, believe in myself. By doing that, I can do the things I like to do. It could be writing a book or script for a movie, creating videos, or starting a business. This is the primary principle of clarity. Does that make sense to you, in connection with what you do? What is one thing you excel at that you would like to turn into your passion?

That is discovering the truth of what a person loves, values, faith, and purpose. As Galileo said once discovered, it is easy to understand the truth. Only by seeking the truth you can gain clarity and a deeper comprehension of yourselves and the situations you face.

I would love to share another story to understand the principles of clarity. I got an opportunity to participate in a panel discussion conducted by MicroMentor, the world's largest volunteer business mentorship program in Dubai in 2023.

There were five panelists including me. It was fascinating to know that almost all the attendees had traveled from various corners of the globe to be part of the session.

Before the session began, the Emcee warmed up the panelists and attendees with an activity. Everyone sat in their chairs as instructed. The Emcee suggested that we had to look at the person sitting next to us and choose one person to act as a mentor and the other as a mentee. She aimed to show that mentoring is not a daunting task, rather a simple, friendly conversation, with the purpose of helping the other person.

She gave us three minutes. Sitting next to me was an engineer from Google who had traveled from the western part of the world to attend the session. We began to talk, and I took on the role of the mentor while she became my mentee. She asked me, "what is clarity coaching? How does it work?" In response, I asked her to share a challenge that she wanted to solve for that week. She explained that she struggled to submit her work on time because various obstacles always seemed to arise.

From our conversation, I found that her biggest challenge was multitasking. In our brief discussion, she was able to pinpoint the purpose behind her actions. She gained clarity on where to direct her focus and where to divert her energy.

As a solution, she decided to leave all the unimportant WhatsApp groups she was a member at that time. In addition, she suggested keeping her mobile in airplane mode to minimize distractions and create undisturbed work time.

From this session, I realized another principle of clarity, which is mindfulness in whatever you do by keeping aside all the distractions.

She knew being in the present and enjoying what she does is the principle of clarity.

Another principle of clarity is being aware of your thoughts, while you are working on your goals.

In the above example, she was ready to find alternative routes and re-adjust her tasks based on that. This is called embracing adaptability. You and I must be coachable. Here she was coachable.

Remember that achieving and maintaining clarity is a dynamic process, and you may find different strategies more effective for your unique circumstances. It's also important to periodically reassess and adjust these principles to align with evolving personal and professional needs.

> ***"Clarity is achieved through understanding and perception, implying that being aware of a situation or concept leads to clarity about it. Clarity is awareness.***

You will achieve diamond-cut clarity when you have a deep understanding of your purpose. That's your 'why', the reason that drives you. Be clear about your life journey. Be clear about your destination.

In essence, the principles of clarity are very simple. Let us check what they are.

- Be curious like a child, observe nature and your surroundings.
- Be open to learning things. Always be ready with an empty cup, so that you can fill it with valuable wisdom and skills.
- Live in the moment and understand the power of being in the present.
- Live intentionally, aligned with your beliefs, values, faith, and purpose.
- Craft a purposeful, compelling goal, and focus on it, by leaving all the distractions behind. Being aware of helpful and unhelpful thoughts.
- Embrace adaptability and readjust your strategies and tactics.

## Call to Action

Which of these principles do you want to focus on more? And rate yourself on where you stand in that particular principle, from 0 to 10.

## CHAPTER 5

# CLARITY AND THE POWER OF NOW

*"Live today, not yesterday. Not tomorrow. Just today. Inhabit your moments. Don't rent them out to tomorrow"*

**– Jerry Spinelli,**
**Children's author**

Clarity is not just about clear thinking; it's also about fully experiencing and appreciating the richness of life. By living in the present, you can immerse yourself in the beauty of the current moment, leading to a more fulfilling and joyous life. We explained this in detail in 'The Principles of Clarity'.

When you focus on the present moment, you eliminate distractions from the past or worries about the future. This heightened concentration allows you to engage more deeply with your current tasks and decisions, fostering mental clarity.

The present moment holds valuable experiences. Embracing and appreciating these moments helps create a positive mindset and a clearer understanding of the richness of your life. Gratitude will be the byproduct.

Focus on the present, for it is the only moment you can act. Create beautiful moments now, whether it's in achieving your goals, nurturing relationships, or increasing your investments and revenue. These actions today lay the foundation for a fulfilling life so that in the future, you can cherish those memories.

With a clear mind, you can focus. But with a cluttered mind, your attention is pulled in many directions. Which mode of living do you prefer? Will you make the most valuable resource, 'time', or carry the weight of overthinking and unwanted thoughts, blocking you from doing what you truly want?

Living in the present allows you to let go of unnecessary mental baggage from the past and future worries. By focusing on the current moment, your mind is free from clutter, promoting clarity of thought.

The present moment offers a clear canvas for decision-making. When you are fully engaged in the 'now', you can assess situations objectively, consider relevant information, and make decisions without being influenced by past regrets or future anxieties.

Being present allows you to be aware of your surroundings, triggers, emotions, and thoughts. This acute awareness provides a clearer understanding of yourself and your environment, fostering overall mental clarity.

Building on the idea of living fully in the present, the Japanese philosophy of Ichi-go ichi-e offers a profound example.

It is a concept often translated as "one moment, one meeting," is a philosophy that reminds us to cherish each moment as unique and unrepeatable. It encourages deep presence and gratitude, knowing that every encounter and experience happens only once in a lifetime.

Their tea ceremony (known as sadō/chadō ('The Way of Tea') or chanoyu) is a cultural activity involving the ceremonial preparation and presentation of matcha, a powdered green tea, in a serene, contemplative setting, highlighting the principles of harmony, respect, purity, and tranquility. The procedure is called 'temae'.

In the context of a tea ceremony, this means fully appreciating the taste of the tea, the atmosphere of the room, and the presence of others, realizing that this exact gathering will never happen again in the same way.

It is a traditional ritual with roots dating back to the 9th century when tea was first introduced to Japan from China. This ceremony was infused with Zen Buddhist principles and emphasized simplicity, rusticity, and spiritual depth.

The ceremony embodies the aesthetic of wabi-sabi, which values simplicity and imperfection and serves as a form of meditation and cultural expression, fostering mindfulness and the appreciation of beauty in everyday actions.

I learned about this concept when I read the book 'Ikigai', and I learned about it more during one of my visits to Expo 2020 Dubai, which happened at Expo City Dubai, UAE.

There, I met a charismatic Japanese leader, who was talking about it. I was really impressed by the way she explained it in such a simple way. She is in her 60s and has learned many things from her experience. I was sitting and listening to her as if I were a kid.

She taught me that this meeting was unique and would never happen again. She believes in "Ichi-go ichi-e". It was a reminder to be fully present and appreciate the fleeting nature of life. Though music and many activities were buzzing around, she taught me to be fully present in this very conversation.

After the Expo, she will be going back to her country and enjoy living in Japan. She told me that after this meeting, we may or may not meet again, however, one thing we can do is cherish that moment.

She took out some attractive things from her bag, her collection of handcrafted pottery, explaining how each piece was made by her or her husband.

While she was showing the pottery, she said "wabi-sabi", the philosophy of finding beauty in life's imperfections. It refers to the concept of time and the idea that every passing moment is unique and can never be repeated in the same way again.

Time is a continuous and ever-flowing process, and every moment that passes is distinct and irreplaceable. Once a moment has passed, it becomes a part of the past and can never be revisited or relived in the same way. Even if we recreate a moment, it will never be the same as the original. I truly believe that you and I must be grateful for every moment we have experienced and those yet to come. Gratitude attracts more meaningful moments into our lives. Gratitude nurtures you with abundance.

Therefore, it is essential to appreciate and make the most of each moment. It is important to live in the present, enjoy the moment, and make the most of the time we have, rather than dwelling on the past or worrying about the future. Such people will experience much more clarity than others. It reminds us that each moment is unique and that we should cherish each encounter as though it may be the last.

I learned the power of 'now' during my leadership journey with Sensei. It is a concept that has profoundly impacted my life, and I hope it inspires you too to live fully and appreciate the beauty of life.

## Call to Action

Think of a moment you fully embraced; one you wish to relive. Recall the small details, the emotions, the inner vibrations, and the joy that made it unforgettable. Write it down in your 'CJ' and read it aloud for a week whenever you need a boost of energy and momentum.

CHAPTER 6

# CLARITY OF PURPOSE: THE PATH TO FULFILLMENT

*"Finding our purpose is what guides us and gives our life meaning. It's also associated with living a longer, healthier and happier life."*

**– Jo Ann Jenkins,**
**Chief Executive Officer (CEO) of AARP**

We have a life, one precious opportunity. However, how do we make it truly meaningful? Living a purpose-driven life is often seen as an unattainable dream. Many believe it's difficult to live with purpose, that identifying it is an overwhelming task requiring strict discipline, leaving no room for fun. People misunderstand the journey, thinking it's a rigid path filled with sacrifice. I believe the answer lies within that very realization. Deep down, in that moment, ask yourself, how do you truly want to be?

In reality, once you discover your true purpose, a sense of ease follows. You feel more relaxed, gain more free time, and even experience more joy in life. Purpose isn't about restriction. It's about alignment. While the road may be long and challenging, embracing your purpose brings clarity, fulfillment, and the freedom to enjoy life fully.

Many of my clients have asked if there is a specific process for discovering their purpose. They said, "I don't know who I am. Sometimes, I feel like I wear different masks, showing different sides of myself, but not truly living."

Losing sight of 'who I am' and 'who I am becoming' happens due to a lack of clarity. Living on autopilot clouds your vision, keeping you from making the effort to break free and grow. By staying committed to what you are doing, by experimenting one step at a time, you are actually uncovering your purpose. It happens only through massive action with deep commitment, moving in the direction your soul seeks. In stagnation, you can't hear your soul's whispers.

Purpose is the meaningful path you carve through action. It unfolds as you commit to serving and adding value to others. You can experiment with multiple activities, if something doesn't bring you fulfillment, let it go. It's better to explore than to remain stuck in uncertainty. When you add value to others' lives, you understand yourself better. You see the impact you create, refining your purpose. Your direction becomes sharper, and deep inside, you feel inspired to keep going. You show up with greater confidence and fulfillment.

Purpose unfolds as you commit to serving and adding value to others. This is the only way you truly evolve.

When you live with purpose, you gain deeper insights into yourself. You see how challenges shape you, guiding your next steps. Your path becomes clearer, and deep inside, you feel excited to do more. You radiate self-confidence and self-esteem.

## Parenting: A Living Example of Evolving Purpose

I can share how my purpose in parenting has unfolded over time and how it continues to evolve through a small event in my life.

When it comes to my purpose as a mother to my kids, it evolves day by day, through my thoughts, actions, and alignment with my values. Parenting is something I was never trained for; it's something I learned from my loved ones. Experience has taught me how to spend time with them, how to guide them, and how to nurture them.

Unlike other areas of my life, where I received formal training, parenting was a journey of self-discovery. As my kids grew, almost in the blink of an eye, I realized this was an area where I needed more learning to truly add value to their lives. I once misunderstood parenting as simply pouring out love, later, I come to realize it's so much more than that.

Whenever my kids chose their own paths, my "mom ego" would surface, making me raise my voice for no real reason. Deep down, I came to understand that from the moment a baby is born, they begin their journey of independent thought, action, and emotion.

At times, I held a prejudiced mindset, unknowingly restricting them from being their true selves. However, once I grasped the concept of clarity, my perspective on parenting became more meaningful.

Working closely with my kids, I realized my parenting strategy had to evolve just as quickly as they grew and changed. They research everything under the sun, challenge ideas, and hold strong opinions. At times, addressing each perspective felt overwhelming. I found myself saying, "I need time, let me check." I had to pause, reflect, and gain clarity on how to guide them to the next level while my own purpose as a parent continued to evolve. I am not the same parent I was when I first started this journey. With my daughter now a teenager, I see that to guide her in every aspect of life, I must first be clear on my own emotional, mental, spiritual, and financial state. Parenting with purpose requires constant self-awareness and growth.

Now, I pause. I reflect. I consciously remind myself to respect them as human beings. I asked myself, why do I need to extend more kindness and compassion towards my kids, why do I need to serve my kids, and how can I serve them far better than this?

I questioned my own patterns: Am I sad, frustrated, or disappointed when I'm triggered or angry? I wrote it all down to identify areas for improvement. I realized that I am the only one who can change this. I must fight for myself to become a more compassionate mom. I asked myself,

They are created with a more advanced brain, which is capable of thinking and acting beyond my own limitations. Their potential is limitless because they are born for this generation. As parents, our perspectives may differ because we are shaped by a different time. The world is advancing, and so are our children. To guide them effectively, we must evolve alongside them.

I still remember when, at the age of four, my daughter asked, "Can I brush my teeth by myself?" A wave of nervousness hit me; how could she manage that alone? At first, I hesitated. Then, instead of saying no, I told her, "Think of each tooth as a strong ally of yours. Name them if you like. Care for them as you would your best friends. Brush the sides, the middle, and in between." I created stories to make it fun.

When my second child shared this thought with me, I had already come to understand that kids only need guidance, they are capable of handling things on their own. Unlike my first experience with my daughter, this time, I was happy to assist my son with more enthusiasm. My thoughts are evolving, and I am still in the process of learning.

My goal as a parent is to guide my children to be authentic, uphold their values, communicate empathetically, and spread joy in their own and others' lives.

## What I Learned from a Visioneer

*Purpose isn't something you find on a single day. It evolves based on what life demands of you.* To truly understand the essence of purpose, one need only look at figures like Nelson Mandela. Enduring 27 years of imprisonment on Robben Island, his unwavering vision for justice and freedom never wavered. His commitment to ending apartheid was driven by a deep sense of clarity.

Mandela said, "I have walked that long road to freedom. I have taken a moment here to rest, to steal a view of the glorious vista that surrounds me, to look back on the distance I have come. But I can only rest for a moment, for with freedom comes responsibilities."

Mandela's story teaches us that true purpose fuels perseverance, even against insurmountable challenges. He used that adverse moment of captivity to reflect and gain perspective on his journey. His passion for equality ignited a movement, inspiring countless individuals to challenge oppression and strive for justice across the globe.

As human beings, you and I must cultivate a burning desire to live and lead, creating beautiful footprints on this planet to leave behind.

When you have fire in your belly, you're like a rocket, propelling yourself toward meaningful impact and lasting change.

## The Path to Purpose

Regardless of the turbulence they encounter along their journeys, it is their strong sense of purpose that propels them forward. These individuals are committed to their convictions and destined paths, tirelessly finding ways to navigate challenges with resilience and patience.

> ***Purpose serves as the unwavering compass guiding remarkable individuals, from prophets to today's successful visionaries.***

No matter the environment, no matter how naysayers react or how others dismiss their ideas, they hold a strong belief in their services, products, or vision. They know their contribution is destined to be worth millions. No matter the long wait for approval or acceptance, they remain steadfast in their belief, knowing their contribution will be worth millions. They work towards their vision. Because purpose is all about others.

Each day, they awaken with courage, enthusiasm, and a passion that fuels their endeavors. Their minds are dedicated to shaping ideas into reality, breathing life into their visions.

## Follow the Thread of What Feels Right

In this section, we will explore how purpose not only defines their actions but also ignites the fire within, inspiring them to turn aspirations into achievements.

I strongly believe that, if you can't figure out your purpose, figure out your passion. Your passion will lead you right to your purpose. Think about the things which energise you. Do that every day.

Your existence isn't a rehearsal. It's not meant to be spent merely watching others live. With clarity and awareness, you can step forward, claim your place, and participate in the life you're meant to lead. Layne Beachley says "If you are doing anything in life that's not fueling your passion to get up on a daily basis, then you are not fulfilling your role as a human being on this planet"

## The Many Faces of Purpose

Talking about purpose, it's important to remember that we each have different purposes in different areas of our lives. There's a purpose for our careers, for our health, for our relationships, and so on. Each area calls for its own focus, values, and goals, and together they shape a balanced, fulfilling life.

This highlights that purpose isn't just a single concept but rather a multifaceted one, touching every important area of life. In order to understand the concept let me share my business purpose here.

> "***My business purpose is to make a huge impact in the world around me, through my writing, coaching, and teaching. Now find out yours.***

You can create a purpose statement for each area of your life that you want to prioritize over the next year. By setting a clear purpose for your career, health, relationships, or any other focus, you'll give yourself direction and meaning in those areas, helping you stay intentional and motivated as you move forward. Understand, you become what you focus. If you focus on your goals, it will expand, and you are going to achieve it.

See, my purpose statement on business and parenting. You can understand that purpose is all about others, whereas passion is about you.

To live a happy and content life, all your actions, big or small, must align with your purpose. If your current vision or goals don't resonate with your inner desires, you might need to reassess and adjust them.

Your purpose is the foundation of your actions. Anything you do, start by asking, "Why" Whether choosing a college subject or a career path, ask yourself, "Why am I doing this?" What is your 'intention' behind it? Your intention must be stronger than your goal.

## Discovering Your Purpose: A Reflective Table

It's not just about what you want to do, It's about why you want to do it. Let your "why" guide your vision. Use this table to reflect deeply on your true motivations behind your aspirations.

| **Write your Purpose here** | **Reasons (Your "Answer")** |
|---|---|
| Why do you want to become an author? | |
| Why do you want to become a pilot? | |
| Why do you want to become a speaker or presenter? | |
| Why do you want to become an AI expert or data scientist? | |
| Why do you want to move to a specific location? | |

| Why do you want to improve your leadership skills? | |
|---|---|
| Why do you want to enhance your writing or communication skills? | |
| Why do you want to learn a new language? | |
| Why do you want to strengthen relationships (with your spouse, kids, parents, or team)? | |
| Why do you want to learn digital marketing or any new skill? | |
| Why do you want to have transition from where you are now to where you want to be? | |

You may fill the column with your purpose and find reasons. If you want to answer these particular challenges, you may fill these, or you can add your own 'purpose' here. I shared some examples to make the concept clear.

## Call to Action

Having clarity on your purpose allows you to stay focused and driven. When you're passionate about what you do, it doesn't feel like work; instead, you find joy and fulfillment in every task. Let me ask you what makes your heart race with excitement and joy. I hope you've taken time to reflect on the table and uncover your purpose. Let that clarity guide every action you take and every goal you pursue.

CHAPTER 7

# PASSION IS ALL ABOUT YOU

---

*"Find something you love to do so much you can't wait for the sun to rise to do it all over again."*

**– Chris Gardner,**
**Entrepreneur, author**

---

Are you passionate about the life you are leading? Are you passionate about the career or job you are having? Passion is all about doing what you love.

Passion often comes from within, fueled by personal interests and desires. It's something you pursue because you genuinely love it, not because of external rewards or expectations.

I've seen many certified doctors practicing with little enthusiasm. "My parents forced me to pursue an MBBS. I had no interest in it, quite the opposite of your story." Now, without their knowledge, I'm conducting training sessions in a completely different field, the one I truly enjoy. It feels effortless, and I'm making a good income from it." My client said.

Another client, professionally an engineer, passionately a photographer, struggled with societal pressure. She was repeatedly told that photography was a tough industry to make money in and not a suitable career for women. Today, she has fully embraced photography and is building her career around her true passion.

It is necessary to figure out your likes and dislikes to lead a happy and inspired life. Watch out for your everyday activities. You can easily understand what you are passionate about. Look at your budget or credit card statement, for clues. Your financial intelligence will tell you more stories about you.

What are the topics you love to learn? Just check out your Google history. Where do you spend more of your energy and time?

What are the topics you often discuss with your close friends? It could be your interests or your passion. Don't ignore it. Check what you can do with those thoughts.

*Here are the 16 questions to ask yourself to find out your passion:*

Write down all your answers in your 'CJ'.

1. Do you start your day with passion?
2. What are the things that motivate you, excite you, or inspire you?
3. Does your work make you fulfilled?
4. What are the things that don't let you sleep?
5. What do you do naturally or extremely well, things that come easily to you and are often challenging for others?
6. What activities do you engage in that provide you with energy, recharge you, or bring you satisfaction and fulfillment?
7. What are the things that make you lose track of time?
8. What are the books you love reading without getting bored? From that, you can identify your passion. Don't you agree?
9. What are the things you would like to do even if you are not paid?
10. What kind of videos do you usually watch?

11. What kind of memes, speeches, podcasts, or shows do you often watch, and which ones spark something in you?
12. What kind of places would you love to visit?
13. Do you always feel sick and tired?
14. What category of people would you like to attract?
15. Where do you see yourself in ten years?
16. Who inspires you? Write down the qualities you admire in them, especially the ones you don't yet have however, feel a strong desire to develop. That longing often points to your true passion.

It is okay, for all these questions you get somewhat similar answers, the more the same answers are there, the higher the chances, and you are very close to identifying your passions. If you have many answers, select five out of them, now give a few more days. Let your subconscious mind work on that.

Then select three out of it, and then stick on one, for the time being. Work on that based on your strength, based on the demand in the marketplace, and check whether it is valuable in the marketplace. If yes is your answer, go with that.

Now you are clear on your passion. Are you happy to take this passion to make a profit and lead a passionate life? Understand, over a period of time, your passion may change, based on your thoughts and wisdom you acquired or the based on the changing need of the world.

## Call to Action

What is the one passion that, if honed diligently, could position you among the industry's elite?

Consider this: In April 2025, Dubai hosted the Global Prompt Engineering Championship, a groundbreaking event during Dubai

AI Week. With a prize pool of AED 1 million, the competition attracted nearly 3,800 participants from 125 countries. After rigorous selection, 24 finalists competed live at AREA 2071 in Emirates Towers, showcasing their skills in categories like Art, Video, Gaming, and Coding.

The winners not only received substantial monetary rewards but also gained international recognition and exposure to industry leaders. I witness this grand event.

This event underscores a pivotal insight: while many may not anticipate such rapid advancements in AI, visionaries do. They recognize emerging fields and invest their efforts accordingly.

Reflect on this scenario. Where does your passion lie? Have you identified a domain where you can excel and contribute meaningfully? The landscape is evolving. Are you ready to be part of the transformation?

## CHAPTER 8

# SEE THE BIG PICTURE

*"Become a positive person by seeing the bigger picture of whatever you dream of doing. Dream big and act big! It's your time to have a bigger image of you!"*

**– Israelmore Ayivor, youth leadership coach**

Do you find yourself primarily caught up in the day-to-day activities, or are you someone who tends to see and appreciate the big picture in various aspects of your life?

To see the big picture in your mind, keep your mind ready to receive the images of what you want in life, for that, you need clarity.

Throughout history, the greatest achievements have come from those who dared to think big. Big-picture thinking means seeing the overall view of a situation or project instead of getting caught up in the details. It's like having an eagle's focus, which is essential for understanding the bigger picture. This kind of thinking helps you keep your end goal in mind while tackling daily tasks. With high clarity and focus, you can stay committed to long-term goals and achieve meaningful results.

Elon Musk envisioned sending rockets to space long before the world believed in him. The Wright brothers dreamed of flying when others thought it was impossible. These pioneering ideas were born from individuals who not only dreamed but believed in themselves before anyone else did.

Those who create history, like them, ask unique questions by seeing the big picture of their ideas. They first visualize those in their mind's eye, and through years of dedicated effort, their thoughts take shape in various models, continuously evolving into a lasting legacy.

To achieve greatness, you must first think big and act as if you've already accomplished your goals. By doing this, your mind begins to adopt those thoughts as reality. In turn, you become what you believe, setting the stage for incredible achievements.

> **"*Clarity is the absence of confusion, chaos, self-doubt, and forgetfulness.***

When seeking clarity on what you want to achieve, a touch of creativity is essential. Let's explore effective methods for gaining clarity and thinking big. Two approaches that stand out for achieving this are writing and mind mapping. Both are powerful tools to refine your goals and expand your vision.

### 1. Write it Down

The ancient method of thinking big was oral tradition and visualization. Before writing became widespread, people used storytelling, symbols, and deep contemplation to envision grand ideas and pass them down.

Now you can write down whatever you feel or want to achieve. It helps you see a bigger perspective. Hold the vision, trust the process. Always keep a journal close, even by your bedside! Ideas can come and go in an instant. Don't let them slip away; give them life. I get the most ideas when I'm in the shower or on the treadmill. If you prefer, you can write it digitally using tools like Google Keep, Apple Notes, Google Docs, or Notion. Still, I believe in the power of pen and paper.

Let us look at how you can write. If you are writing it down you need to understand that you write it in running letters, which we use every day. Use present tense. When you write your goals or vision in the present tense, it tells your mind that it's already happening.

This activates your subconscious, boosts belief, and helps align your thoughts, feelings, and actions toward making it real. It's a powerful psychological trick that shifts you from "maybe someday" to "I'm already living it," which strengthens focus, motivation, and confidence.

When you write, give yourself permission to dream. Use multi-color pens to make it more creative. Be creative as a kid, little children know nothing of judgement and scarcity. Thinking big is a learnable skill, with practice, by chasing your dreams.

You may go for a walk or visit a new coffee shop. Being in a different setting may help your brain to identify different possibilities than you would in your usual environment.

## 2. Mind Mapping

It is a powerful tool that unlocks creativity and enhances clarity, allowing you to visually organize your thoughts and ideas. It transforms abstract concepts into tangible plans, making it easier to see connections and pathways to your goals.

With this dynamic approach, you can manifest your vision more effectively.

Now, let's look at what you need to start your mind mapping process

- Colorful Pens: Gather a variety of colorful pens, and make sure to include some scented ones for extra fun!
- Paper or Journal: Always have paper or a journal with you to visualize your ideas whenever inspiration strikes.
- Candy: Treat yourself with chocolate, select the flavor you loved as a kid to reconnect with your inner child as you create!

Girls: Braid your hair and wear your formal dress.

Boys: Rock some cool sunglasses, wear a favorite shirt, or wear your smartwatch. Even if you are at home, sit as if you are sitting at your office desk, or in any professional setup.

Take a moment to pause and surrender for the next five to six minutes. Begin by breathing fully, inhaling through your nose to invite in all the joy and peace you seek. Then, exhale slowly through your mouth, releasing any worries and stress.

Repeat this process three times, allowing each breath to clear tension and guide you into a state of openness and allowance. Embrace the stillness as you connect with your inner calm.

### How to Draw your Mind map

Start by writing your name and objective in the center circle. Then, let your ideas flow freely. Use separate branches radiating from the center to break down different aspects of your main idea. Based on the given diagram, fill each circle with clear, detailed points. You can add more branches as needed to create a vivid, complete picture. Use different colors for each branch to visually organize your thoughts and highlight connections for maximum clarity.

Always keep in mind: without a proper date, the dream is never going to be met.

## Who - What- Why - Where - When

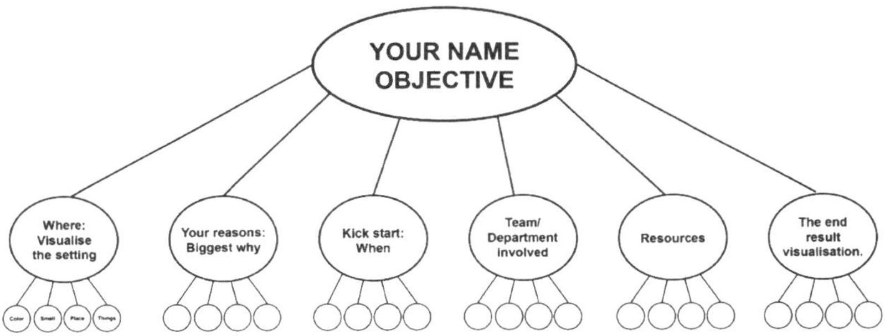


Mind mapping helps organize information effectively and stimulates creative thinking by visually representing relationships between ideas.

## Examples of Mind mapping

Draw the model the way you want to create your mind maps.

- **Business:** Serving who? What does your customer look like? What challenges are you solving? Be creative, based on your imagination. Drill down!!
- **Vacation:** Where to?

When: In the Spring/ Summer/ Winter?

Who will you go with? Mention your accountability partners here

Where will you stay? How will this make you feel? Explain each deep feeling associated with it.

- **Car:** What color? What does the steering wheel feel like? What's the smell? Pay in cash or finance? You need to feel the whole experience, as if you owned the car, were an entrepreneur, or had already visited the place.

Replace negative self-talk with powerful affirmations and social accountability. When your mind is focused on your dreams, you don't have time for the many self-doubts that block them, and getting clear is the first step.

Your thinking and your vision for your dream have to be clear in every detail. Do not trust luck and hope. Do not wish for a magic wand, which will make your life beautiful. Wishing is not enough. Plan it well in advance with clarity. If you have clarity, you will definitely hit the bull's eye.

Looking forward to seeing you in action, living the life you are dreaming of.

### The Magnifying Glass Effect

Imagine, you are outside on a beautiful sunny day, a dried leaf in one hand and a magnifying glass in the other, which focuses the sun's rays onto the leaf, what will happen? The leaf catches the fire and starts burning. That is the power of focus.

My daughter used to do this when she was a child. When I was a fifth grader my teacher taught me this. Have you ever done this? Most of us, right?

The sunlight focused on a glass will make it burn. Just as a magnifying glass can focus sunlight to ignite a dried leaf, a mind map concentrates scattered thoughts into a single vision, sparking action and transformation. You need the clarity and focus of the magnifying glass.

## Call to Action

What's your strategy for dreaming big? Have you created your mind map? How was your experience? Once you have done it, give yourself a high five by looking into the mirror. Congratulations!

CHAPTER 9

# AFFIRMATIONS FOR THE 'PERSON OF CLARITY'

*"Affirmations are like planting seeds in the ground. The more you plant, the more you harvest."*

**– Louise Hay, author**

During my college days, when I was in a state of confusion, no one taught me the power of affirmations. It wasn't until much later that I discovered how great leaders like Vishen Lakhiani had been practicing affirmations, mindfulness, and visualization since their teenage years. I wondered, how advanced they were in shaping their mindset from such a young age.

However, upon reflection, I realized that I had witnessed a form of affirmation all along, through my mother. During her toughest times, she carried an unshakable sense of positivity. Perhaps, without even knowing it, she was affirming herself every day. I especially remember how she navigated the emotional turbulence of menopause. Looking back, I now believe that something within her, a quiet, unwavering self-assurance, helped her push through.

She always radiated gratitude. She talked to her creator constantly, infusing every part of her day with faith and positivity. I heard her prayers, observed her resilience, I too started practicing her habits intentionally.

The French psychologist Émile Coué observed that his patients often recovered faster when he encouraged them to expect healing. He developed what he called optimistic autosuggestions—positive statements that patients repeated to themselves, reinforcing their belief in recovery.

Affirmations aren't just words; they are a force that shapes your reality. And perhaps, my mother had been practicing them all along, without ever calling them affirmations.

In this chapter, we focus on a few affirmations to practice for 90 days, helping you become a better 'person of clarity.' Each day, you'll find yourself growing better and better, moving into a more relaxed state of mind. By consistently practicing these affirmations, you'll find it easier to handle stress, anxiety, and uninspired thoughts.

Your mind is often jampacked with worries, anxieties, stress, and overloaded tasks, leaving no clarity on how to move forward. This lack of clarity hampers your ability to complete important tasks. With 60,000 to 80,000 thoughts passing through your mind each day, (an average calculation) it becomes your responsibility to analyze and manage these thoughts effectively. If you give the right message to your brain, it can accomplish great things.

Decluttering your mind allows you to analyze situations better and become more productive.

It is your responsibility to feed your mind with positive and affirming thoughts to eliminate unhelpful ones. Otherwise, unhelpful thoughts will dominate, leading to stagnation and disappointment. Positive thoughts help declutter your mind, resulting in organized and productive thinking.

Focus on helpful, positive, or empowering thoughts, whichever term resonates with you. Celebrate small victories and give yourself a pat on the back for even for minor successes. This will keep you motivated throughout the day.

To begin, sit in an undisturbed place and, if you wish, close your eyes. Focus on your breath. You might hear sounds from your surroundings, and that's okay. Gently bring your mind back to your breath. No matter how challenging it feels initially, continuous practice will help you achieve a clear state of mind.

Start by taking two slow, deep breaths in through your nose and out through your mouth. Feel the calmness as you begin this journey of self-discovery and empowerment. Let your words guide you toward a more positive and purposeful life. Read aloud the affirmations below.

*I am a person of clarity; I am focused on my goals and visions.*

*Clarity is my inward eye.*

*Clarity is my inner compass.*

*I breathe in clarity; I breathe out stress.*

*I breathe in clarity; I breathe out anxiety.*

*I breathe in clarity; I breathe out self-doubt.*

*I breathe in clarity; I breathe out worry.*

*I breathe in clarity; I breathe out overwhelm.*

*My mind is so clear, like a diamond. I can visualize all that I desire clearly.*

*I am focused on nurturing clarity and cultivating deeper awareness in all that I do.*

*I release all anxiety, stress, and worries, letting them fade away.*

*I am open to receiving calmness and clarity.*

*I trust my intuition completely. It is my lighthouse, guiding me towards the right path.*

*I am confident in my ability to overcome my limiting beliefs.*

*I am confident in my ability to liberate myself from my fears.*

*I am able to remove all obstacles.*

*I am worthy.*

*I deserve success.*

*I live each day with passion and purpose.*

*I remain steadfast in my values, no matter how challenging the circumstances are.*

*My principles guide me, even when the path is difficult.*

*I am in charge of my character and behavior.*

*I see abundance everywhere.*

*I always have enough money for what I set for myself.*

*I attract money.*

*I consistently attract all the right people to help me grow my business*

*I am committed to being intentional in every act that I do.*

*I release old habits that no longer serve me.*

## Calmness and Inner Strength

Each week, spend time reflecting on your progress. Has your mind become clearer? Are you more focused on your goals? How do you feel after practicing the affirmations for clarity?

Use your 'CJ' as a space for personal insight, capturing the moments of growth and transformation. It will also serve as a powerful reminder of how far you've come.

### Living a Life of Clarity

At the end of these 90 days, you will have established yourself as a 'person of clarity.' By clearing the mental clutter and focusing on affirming thoughts, you'll notice that you handle stress with more ease, make decisions with greater confidence, and live with a sense of purpose and awareness.

Continue practicing these affirmations beyond the 90 days, making them a natural part of your life. Clarity is not a destination but a journey, and each day offers an opportunity to deepen your awareness and move closer to your highest self. "If visualization is the movie you play in your mind, affirmation is the script you speak into reality."

### Call to Action

Now, start your daily tasks with greater clarity, awareness, and prioritization. Declutter unhelpful thoughts whenever you need to regain focus. Life can often feel like standing on a treadmill, there may be moments when you feel stuck or overwhelmed.

As a person of clarity, it is your responsibility to step back, evaluate the situation or thoughts, and realign yourself with purpose. Remember, finding clarity is an ongoing process, and each time you pause to reassess, you grow stronger in your ability to navigate life with confidence and wisdom.

CHAPTER 10

# A ROADMAP IS YOUR GUIDE TO CLARITY

Life is a series of events, challenges, ups, and downs. You and I aspire to be our own commanders, so we must first master clarity, clarity of purpose, direction, and action. Understanding the key objectives of your life, in each area and creating clear plans will make your journey much smoother.

Create a visual roadmap of your goals and milestones. Stick it on your wall or set it as your screensaver. With every glance, pause to ponder, reroute, and redefine your journey. A daily reminder to keep you focused and motivated on your journey. Update it weekly or monthly, because clarity is not just a destination; it's an evolving path of growth and self-discovery.

Just like my then 18-year-old nephew, who is a backpacker who beautifully illustrated his travel dreams on his wall with his bike, pursuing 60% of them, you and I can benefit from visualizing our goals.

His determination and will power reminds us that each milestone is a step closer to fulfillment, encouraging you and I to keep moving forward.

As you create your roadmap, remember that it's not just about reaching a destination, it is embracing the journey and the adventures it brings along the way.

A roadmap is a strategic plan that outlines the steps or milestones needed to achieve a goal or vision.

> ***It's like a visual guide that shows the direction, priorities, and key actions required to reach a specific destination, whether in business, personal development or project management.***

In business, for example, a roadmap might show phases of a product launch. In personal development, it could be map out steps toward a major goal, like acquiring new skills or achieving fitness objectives.

Roadmaps help keep the end goal in sight and provide a sequence of achievable steps, making complex plans more manageable and focused. You can see the big picture, exactly like you have a GPS, in your journey.

Having a well-defined plan helps you to instill a sense of direction and empowers you to journey with purpose, unlocking the doors to personal growth, fulfillment, and a life rich in meaning.

Have you ever thought about how a simple roadmap could be the key to unlocking your success? Just like my nephew's visual representation of his dreams, a clear path can guide you toward your goals.

Clarity provides a roadmap to success, productivity, growth, happiness, and joy. Clarity is essential in creating a roadmap because it defines purpose, direction, and actionable steps, all critical for successful outcomes.

You now know that clarity is related to your life, your dreams, goals, and aspirations. It has a vital role in your personal growth and development. A roadmap serves as a strategic plan, offering guidance to navigate challenges and uncertainties.

By breaking down your goals into manageable tasks, the roadmap becomes a practical tool for progress. Regularly reviewing and adjusting the map ensures you stay on track toward achieving your aspirations. When you don't have direction, confusion, uncertainty, indecision, and a sense of aimlessness may arise.

Now let us discuss what could be the results of not having a road map.

> ***A roadmap will allow you to travel with intention and reflection, providing a clear path through life's complexities.***

It becomes your guiding companion, helping you navigate challenges, make informed decisions, and stay focused on your destination.

## The Absence of a Roadmap can Lead to

**Waste of time:** Without a clear roadmap, you risk losing focus, drifting down unproductive paths, wasting time on distractions, missing crucial opportunities, and neglecting more important goals, ultimately failing to reach what truly matters.

**Waste of energy:** Without a roadmap, you risk wasting energy and resources by juggling too many things, feeling overwhelmed, and taking unnecessary detours.

**Waste of money:** Without a clear roadmap, projects can face delays, misaligned accountability, and misallocated resources, causing costs to rise and funds to be wasted. A roadmap ensures efficient use of resources, timely progress, and accountability to meet objectives within budget.

It also helps to ensure that resources are used as efficiently as possible and that the business is well-positioned to take advantage of potential opportunities.

For example, If you don't have a clear strategy for your program and its target audience when running Facebook ads, it means you don't have a clear roadmap. Then you are going to lose a lot of money.

***Not having a roadmap, you may reach somewhere else:*** Imagine you plan to meet a friend but end up at the wrong café because you didn't check the address. Without clear directions, you arrive somewhere unintended. Similarly, without a roadmap, your efforts can go off course, leading to wasted resources and missed goals. A clear plan keeps you on track.

Successful people always know what to do because they have a clear roadmap— a purposeful plan that aligns daily actions with long-term goals. Without this, uncertainty takes over, leading to indecision, procrastination, and loss of confidence. Without direction, it's hard to measure progress or stay motivated, and you risk getting lost both figuratively and literally.

A roadmap acts as your game plan, outlining the steps needed to reach your destination. It provides structure, focus, and permission to take massive action. Without it, you're left reacting to daily distractions rather than steering toward meaningful success.

Hence, I encourage you to take a few moments to formulate a personal plan for your own life. Draw it in your journal, the way you can. Then work towards your goal.

## Call to Action

Have you ever crafted a roadmap for your goals before? Reflect on your past experiences. Did you achieve them? Assess where you stand right now.

Envision your ultimate destination. Where do you want to go in life? What's the farthest you can imagine going? Dare to dream big and let your vision guide you.

What action will you commit to take right now to move closer to the life you envision?

CHAPTER 11

# FINDING CLARITY AMIDST THE CHAOS

*"Clarity will come as you find calmness in chaos."*

**– Sydney Banks,**
**Philosopher and author**

In today's fast-paced world, it's essential to cultivate clarity to lead a happy, relaxed, and productive life.

It is time to pause and step out of autopilot, instead of being controlled by constant phone pings and email alerts. You often stay alert because of nonstop notifications, too much digital content and mental noise.

During ancient times, people were in constant touch with nature and listened to nature more often. They were highly social beings, compared to this digital world. Research shows that listening to birdsong can have a significant positive impact on mental health. Now let me share a story to understand it.

One of my clients faced a challenge: working in shifts disrupted his sleep patterns, leaving him restless and unsure of how to get sufficient rest. During his free time at night, he found himself aimlessly walking, surfing the internet, or watching Netflix. Unfortunately, this routine led to stagnation rather than growth. He started complaining. He started blaming his family.

The lack of clarity on how to address his sleep issues resulted in feelings of depression, stress, anxiety, and self-sabotage.

This isn't just one person's story. It's a challenge many of us face in the digital age. While solutions exist, they only work when approached with intentional effort, helping to break habitual patterns. A digital detox can provide much-needed relief. Practicing habits like, use autopilot mode or enable a grey screen to make your phone less engaging. This reduces distractions by making videos and images less attractive, helping you lose interest and put your phone down more easily. Or you can keep your phone away from your room also can make a significant difference.

Rejuvenate your body with a cold or hot shower. Sit in stillness to connect with your deeper feelings, the secrets you only share with yourself, the pangs and agonies that shape your inner world.

Reach a state of mindfulness through guided meditation, which helps filter the information that reaches you from the outside world. Visualize the life you want to live; it will give you motivation. Practice affirmations too.

Constantly re-educate and reinvent yourself. You need to sharpen and invest in the development of your competencies.

You can learn the things that you didn't know till yesterday, you can unlearn the things that you are practicing imperfectly and you can re-learn the things that you learned earlier, however not practicing them right now.

When clarity escapes you, you tend to resort to blaming, complaining, justifying, and even lashing out at those around us, like my client did. On the other hand, when you possess clarity, you find inner peace. With this peace, you effortlessly extend kindness and understanding to others. The outcome is beautiful. Refer the subtopic, benefits of clarity.

Without clarity, you often find yourself saying, "If only I lived in a better place," or "If only I hadn't inherited such a bad temper," among other things. These thoughts may offer temporary relief, however without clarity, you engage in a cycle of blame and generalization.

Individuals who fail to set objectives for themselves often operate on autopilot, lacking intentionality in their actions.

To optimize productivity and clarity in life, it's essential to design your days, weeks, months, and years effectively. Take time to analyze where you may be wasting time, whether it's excessive Netflix binging, online shopping sprees, or endlessly scrolling through sales.

*Your mind will answer most questions if you learn to sit with yourself and wait for the answer.*

> **"*Ask yourself, can I help someone, so that I feel excited for the remaining hours of the day?*"**

Develop the courage to say 'no' to things, activities that are not going to serve you, habits that are not going to serve you, or the courage to say 'no' to people who drain your energy and time.

### How to Say 'NO'?

Imagine the life you aspire to in a specific aspect, such as "health." For instance, if you have a chronic condition like diabetes, take proactive measures to manage it. Avoid sugary foods and beverages, refined grains, fried potatoes, and processed meats to maintain better health and well-being.

What can you do to lead a happy life? If you can do five push-ups a day, go for it, write one paragraph every single day.

For these, you don't have to lock your time. If you do more than two tasks, that is your bonus, celebrate it. Say aloud "I am a Winner". It is up to you if you want to be in a clear state of mind, or a contaminated one. The choice is yours.

Another area where you need to say 'No' is when you have to face energy suckers and time suckers, or a situation where you feel that may pull you down. Or someone gives you a task, where your plate is already full. If you are in your work, say no to other activities, even if it is your family members.

### Call to Action

Identify situations where you struggle to say no. How does saying yes to these situations affect your productivity or well-being?

Write down three ways to practice saying no confidently.

CHAPTER 12

# WHY DO YOU FEEL STUCK AND HOW TO BREAK FREE?

> ***"Embrace the power of being a 'Person of Clarity' (PC) by taking a break from your Personal Computer (PC) and other devices. Disconnect to reconnect with yourself in silence, turning moments alone into the brilliance of clarity."***

Being a Person of Clarity (PC) is a choice. A PC is someone who possesses a clear and focused understanding of themselves, their goals, visions, strengths, weaknesses, distractions, time-sucking activities, and their surroundings. Such an individual is capable of making well-informed decisions, maintaining sharp focus, maintaining a sense of purpose, and navigating challenges with a clear and unclouded perspective.

When I faced technical issues or a lack of professional assistance in my book writing process, I took a moment to pause and identified the obstacles. I wrote down everything and brainstormed all possible options to get my work done in the best way possible. This process often revealed new opportunities. I reached out to the right people, and I got a better outcome than before.

## Reasons You Feel Stuck

1. **Lack of Clarity**
   Clarity isn't just about knowing what you want to achieve. It is also about recognizing what you need to eliminate.
   Even those at the top of the corporate ladder, with impressive titles and achievements, often feel a subtle void there comes the importance of sitting beside you for a while. In Linchpin, Seth Godin emphasizes that the most valuable people in any organization are not just following a script. They bring emotional labor, creativity, and connection. But to do that, they must be clear on who they are, what they stand for, and the unique value they bring. Without clarity, even the most talented become replaceable.
   True clarity helps you shed the noise, find your rhythm, and feel grounded, peaceful and fulfilled in life.
2. **Lack of Courage**
   You need to have the courage to take the first step. The courage to drive your life to the next step and you must have the courage to sit in the cockpit.
3. **Lack of Competency**
   Sitting in the cockpit will not help until you know how to take the flight to the right destination. To reach 'where you want to reach', you need

> ***"Empower your professional journey by putting it through the crucible of practice. Competency is the combination of knowledge, attitude, skill, and habit."***

to sharpen your competency, day by day, by putting it into practice.

Through consistent and challenging practices, one can enhance and strengthen their skills or competencies.

4. **Lack of Consistency**

   You need to maintain a proper pace, only then you will be able to reach your destination. Keep driving to be successful.

5. **Lack of Concentration**

   Clarity gives you the target where as concentration pulls the arrow. Until you finish one thing, be fully present with it. Do it with complete concentration.

6. **Lack of Communication**

   Communication and clarity must go hand in hand to spread joy and happiness. Every time you speak, you open the door to endless possibilities. You can influence, uplift, and connect, or confuse, discourage, and distance.

   The way a mother speaks to her children not only shapes the atmosphere in the home but also echoes in how those children interact with the world around them. Her words have the power to nurture confidence, trust, and love or to create uncertainty and emotional distance.

   Lacking communication skills in roles like parent, manager, or CEO can cause serious problems. Poor communication leads to

   a) Escalated conflict

   b) Feeling unseen or misunderstood

   c) Loneliness or stress

   d) Difficulty setting and achieving goals.

7. **Lack of Creativity**

   If you are stuck, you won't look for solutions or challenge yourself, or you won't see the possibilities.

Life may throw curve balls at you. However, you must have the spirit shield with you. Of course, there are obstacles. You need to find options. Then opportunities that you've never thought of that bring new and better outcomes.

8. **Lack of Commitment**

   Commitment is key. Drive until you reach your destination. If you are committed, you won't stop when you are tired; you stop only when you are done. Commitment means pursuing your goal relentlessly, even when the path is difficult. If you are truly committed, you won't settle for what's easy; instead, you'll find ways to overcome obstacles and achieve your objectives.

   You'll go the extra mile, including seeking out the right person for clear guidance and support, without worrying about stretching your limits.

9. **Lack of Good Character**

   Character is the foundation of success. Only when your character is good and you are 100 percent committed, your vision or purpose can be achieved. The state of feeling stuck and character are connected because addressing challenges requires and showcases one's resilience, determination, and integrity. You will get to know more about your true character when you get stuck and need help, however, nobody is there beside you to help.

   Always value yourself by asking questions like what you need to improve, what you need to learn, what needs to change, what you need to stop, and who can help you.

10. **Lack of Leadership**

    Without leadership, individuals may feel adrift. There is no clear goal or roadmap, if you lack leadership. You need leadership when you get stuck to provide direction, motivation, and solutions to handle challenges effectively. As John C Maxwell said, "Everything rises and falls on leadership" which means the success or failure of any organization or person or endeavor heavily depends on the quality of its leadership.

11. **Fear of being Judged**

    Investing too much stock in what other people will think or any negativity they impose on your decision can be paralyzing. Go with your intuition. You can't shut another's mouth. You can't control the people around you. Trust me, if you fall into this category, you're spending too much time on others. If you redirected that time toward sharpening your skills, learning something new, or refining your thoughts, you would have gone the extra mile or beyond!

12. **Comparing Yourself to Others**

    Keep in mind that "Comparison kills your joy." Compare your past achievements with your today's achievements to motivate yourself, and compare your growth, your potential, and your future.

13. **You Feel Disconnected from Your Values**

    If your values are uncertain, or not strong enough, you feel disconnected from your thoughts. Guiding an employee after a costly mistake, giving credit to the team in success, taking blame in failure, valuing people over profit, and listening patiently to your kids and spouse even in disagreement, are all simple, powerful ways to uphold values, which are your strong pillars.

14. **Not Ready to Change**

    Always be ready to change with the changing market demands. You must be adaptable to the situation. I have seen many youngsters who visit different countries, to make a living, end up sleeping in a rented room, with one meal a day. They have no clarity on why they went there or how to chase their dream.

In most cases, people don't realize they got stuck. They firmly believe they are doing the right thing and have already exhausted all possible efforts.

15. **Lack of Hope for the Future**

    Your thoughts are powerful tools. They can send you in the direction you want to head or keep you pinned in one place. Set a clear vision to move forward.

16. **You're Overwhelmed or Burnt Out**

    You could be overwhelmed by your circumstances and life events. Or the possibility and pressure of your next move could cause you to stress. Whether it's over your past or potential future, overwhelm can be hard to overcome. Focus on the present.

    If you are overwhelmed with the tasks at hand, you need to chunk it down and give yourself some time to pause and reflect.

17. **The Narrative You Create in Your Head**

    There might be plenty of reasons to make a change and plenty of equally strong reasons not to change because you are not ready to take responsibility, you want to sit on the couch as merely a watcher, not a player.

    For example, you may want to change your job and also really value your free time. What do you do? You perhaps, neglect the dream of changing your job. This type of pattern can lead you into a vicious cycle that doesn't lead anywhere.

18. **You're in Your Comfort Zone**

    You may know what you need to do to become unstuck but feel uncomfortable moving forward. If it's the first time that you're testing a skill or behavior, for example, you might not know what to do exactly. You could be fighting self-doubt or perfectionism. Fear of making a mistake or fear of having a less-than-perfect result can hold you back.

19. **Imbalance in different Areas of Your Life**
    Feeling stuck often arises from an imbalance in various aspects of life, creating disharmony in the wheel of life. This imbalance may stem from neglecting certain areas such as career, relationships, or personal well-being. Addressing the issues and restoring equilibrium in these areas of life can contribute to a sense of fulfillment and progress.

## Call to Action

Find out the things that make you feel like they are holding you back. Identify those and write them down. What are the remedial measures you are going to take? Whatever solutions you have, start acting immediately. Show a sense of urgency.

# CHAPTER 13

# BREAKING THE CHAINS; AVOID THESE PITFALLS!

*"Growth is painful. Change is painful. But nothing is as painful as staying stuck where you do not belong."*

**– N. R. Narayana Murthy, billionare and philanthropist**

We discussed a lot about clarity and how to find clarity. How to break the stagnation into a fruitful moment, where you are joyful and focusing on your big dreams. You need to understand that the only place you are stuck is in your head. Whatever change you want to make, whatever risk you want to take, sit, ponder, plan, and do it.

Plant a seed of clarity, to your brain. It is like you are enriching your mind with good thoughts, like a gardener nourishing his plants, or like a gemologist heating the diamond to very high temperatures in the presence of a specific atmosphere, such as nitrogen or air.

During this heating process, the crystal lattice structure of the diamond is disrupted, and the carbon atoms rearrange themselves, allowing for the formation of a new crystal structure. This can result in changes to the diamond's shape or even its color. The outcome can be unpredictable, just like this process, reprogram your thoughts.

This chapter is about breaking free from that cycle, shaking things up, and discovering new possibilities. Let's explore ways to free ourselves from feeling 'stuck', create a pure gem-like state of mind, and breathe fresh life into our routines. Welcome to the quest to break free from the chain and embrace change!

When you feel stuck in a rut, keep these in mind:

### Victim of Negative Self-talk

Say, "I can see things clearly" instead of "I am feeling stuck."

When you feel uninspired, ask yourself: "What is the gift within me?"

When life feels disappointing, reflect: "What is the one lesson I have learned in this situation?"

And when everything seems to be falling apart, pause and ask: "What is the blessing here?", Tell yourself, that you are a person of clarity.

No need to over-identify with the situation.

You need to let go of emotional attachment to outcomes and focus on the present moment without being overly influenced by past experiences or future expectations.

At times you might feel stuck, but the next moment you might feel tired, delighted, or have several emotions. It's okay to show your emotions. However, don't be there for too long.

If one door closes, another one opens Infront of you. Tell yourself, there's no need to compare myself to others or any situation. "My path is unique, and opportunities are always within reach."

### Self-criticism

Be empathetic to yourself. Communicating within yourself compassionately will help you reduce stress; thus, you can reflect on the actual situation.

### Beat Yourself Up

Avoid fixating solely on the stuck area, maintain a broader perspective of your life. A limited perspective keeps you stuck in the same position, trapped within a frame.

Remember that each situation that makes you feel stuck is just one part of your life. It is just one event. For example, if you feel stuck at work, spend some time appreciating what is good about your health or relationships. Embrace the blessing within you to open your mind and eyes, bringing a dramatic shift in your energy. Gratitude journaling is the best way to practice at this stage until tears roll down.

### Not Taking Ownership of the Mistake

You need to take ownership of your mistakes. Inner games and excuses like, justification, complaints, and blame are not suitable for you, instead take ownership of your mistakes, it's human. Don't doubt your ability to handle your decisions. Trust your intuition. Trust your abilities.

### Blaming Others

You don't live in a vacuum, and others' decisions and actions can impact your lives. However, dwelling on them isn't productive.

And remember that you're ultimately in charge of many aspects of your personal and professional life. If you are accountable, there is no room for justification, blame, complaints, or arguments.

## Doubting Your Ability to Handle Your Decisions

If you find yourself struggling with a decision between two options, consider rating them. Permit yourself to choose by assigning each a rating, and the higher-rated option becomes your best decision.

Unlike a ship that's stranded, a car stuck in the mud, or a fallen tree blocking a river's path, the particular 'stuckness' of humans can be a state of mind or perspective.

Choose to see your situation through a different lens and see what opens up for you. When you have clarity and peace of mind, you don't tend to be caught up in the form of contaminated thinking.

I love these lines of Sydney Banks recordings from 'Mind and Insecurity' which was recorded in the 1970s.

*"The mind doesn't belong to you and me.*
*You just borrow it, because the mind is a very spiritual thing.*
*It's non-tangible.*
*You can't possibly find out what it is.*
*You can't show anybody what it is.*
*Because it's a spiritual thing.*
*It's a spiritual energy, which has knowledge of literally all things."*

I truly enjoyed these lines.

In 'The Pursuit of Happyness', a heartwarming true story, we follow Chris Gardner (Will Smith), a struggling salesman facing financial hardships and homelessness. Despite the adversities, Chris remains determined to create a better life for himself and his son. The film beautifully portrays the power of resilience, perseverance, and the pursuit of one's dreams.

*"Increasing clarity is the inevitable result of a transformation in your understanding of how life works"*

**– Jamie Smart,**
**Sunday Times Bestselling Author**

# CHAPTER 14

# THE QUALITIES OF PEOPLE WITH GREATER CLARITY

*"Clarity of mind means clarity of passion, too; this is why a great and clear mind loves ardently and sees distinctly what it loves"*

**– Blaise Pascal (1623-1662)**
**Mathematician and philosopher**

Let us check what are the qualities of the individual with 'diamond cut clarity'.

> ***Clarity is no accident. It emerges through reflection, addressing your questions, awakening, eliminating distractions, learning, studying, focusing and most importantly, a deep love for knowing yourself with true trust.***

- People who have clarity always have a clear destination in mind, even if they're not sure about the exact path to get there. They always have a big picture in mind, no matter where they are in the process, or what they are doing. They see everything from a wider perspective. They know exactly where they are and what they want to be. They have high vision and they are very flexible.

> *"Vision is the ability to talk about the future with such clarity, that it is as if we are talking about the past"*
>
> **– Simon Sinek**

- People with clarity are driven by passion. At any cost, even if it is too cold, they are ready to wake up early in the morning, start with rituals, and start on time with passion. They are not driven by fluctuating moods.

One of my friends, an Ayurvedic doctor by profession, who had been to the Himalayas twice, told me that at three AM, he had to wake up in freezing temperatures. He broke some glaciers to wash his body. He has the guts to do that. Here I am just talking about the courage or mentally strong mindset, not about how it is harmful to the environment. He was very clear about his purpose.

- People who are clear about what they want don't let fear stop them. They stay positive and focus on doing things that help them move forward. Their minds are like tidy rooms, making it easier for them to imagine success and deal with problems without getting overwhelmed.

- They excel in clear thinking, transparent communication, and decisive action. Their ability to articulate ideas and make informed choices sets them apart, fostering genuine connections and contributing positively in various spheres.

Their clear thinking is facilitated by a calm mind, not a stormy one. This mental tranquility enables them to process information effectively, make sound decisions, and communicate their ideas clearly and confidently.

- They visualize themselves in the greater positions they aspire to achieve.

**The Power of Visualisation Stories**

Sensei said that he had no knowledge of visualization or goal-setting in the 1990s, yet with remarkable mental clarity, he clearly visualized exactly what he wanted and went on to win the award. Sensei mentioned that he achieved this even before he had learned about the power of visualization, goal-setting, or meditation. How come it happened?

He visualized himself succeeding, in landing a powerful kick, dodging an opponent's attack, or scoring points. He saw himself in the same position, he saw exactly what happened in the ring in his mind, as it had happened many years in his mind, with crystal clear clarity.

He mentally rehearsed each karate move, focusing on the perfect execution. He won 8 times, a world record. He broke his own world records.

Now let us take the example of Michael Phelps, one of the greatest swimmers of all time. He attributes much of his success to the power of visualization. From a young age, Phelps learned to mentally rehearse his races, vividly imagining every stroke, turn, and finish. Each night before bed and every morning before practice, he visualized himself swimming flawlessly and standing on the podium. This mental preparation became a crucial part of his routine.

Phelps's coach, Bob Bowman, emphasized the importance of this technique, encouraging him to visualize not only perfect races but also potential challenges, such as a goggle malfunction or a false start. This practice ensured Phelps remained calm and focused, even when things didn't go as planned.

During the 2008 Beijing Olympics, Phelps's goggles filled with water during the 200-meter butterfly. Instead of panicking, he relied on his visualization training, counting his strokes and maintaining his pace. He won the race and set a world record, demonstrating the incredible power of visualization.

Manoj Vasudevan said the same in his book. He could visualize himself in the Toastmasters' manual, and he could visualize the exact heaviness of his championship trophy.

- Mental clarity allows leaders to fight against all odd challenges and struggles in their own way. Because they know that trusting themselves is the foundation of every action. They anticipate things.
- People with clarity have a continuous focus only on their goals. They are ready to strategize their goal. Instead of attempting for a huge leap, they simplify the process and make sure they will not give up in any circumstances.

Once they decide on something, they bravely take action and follow through with determination. With their clear and focused minds, they are unstoppable. Even if they make mistakes along the way, they see them as opportunities to learn and grow. Courage is their best tool. They understand the dangers of procrastination and refuse to delay their responsibilities, knowing that dreams can slip away if they do. You always need to press the start button, not the pause button in your life. All these made them realize that success requires huge personal sacrifices.

With clarity, they understand the importance of taking small, consistent steps toward their goals, yielding significant results over time.

- People with clear minds know the importance of focusing on their strengths, rather than wasting time and energy to focus on their weaknesses.

'What is the least I can spend to get help' is absolute crap for them. Instead, they focus on return on investment. They ask 'What's the most I can afford, to get the very best help possible?'

- With clarity, they know the importance of surrounding themselves with quality people. My mentor, always says, that when he adds people to his tribe, he adds 'Only Quality People'(OQP)
- Individuals with diamond-cut clarity are ready to serve their customers by asking what they want. They put themselves in their customer's shoes, not what products/services are available to them. They are ready to be creative and innovate new things, if the market demands it, or based on their customers' deep pains or challenges.
- With clear minds, they're willing to take calculated risks and show remarkable determination.

Calculated risk means taking a risk after carefully considering and understanding the potential consequences and benefits.

For example, if you want to quit your current job, it's essential to take certain precautions first. You can't just quit immediately without having a new job lined up because this could leave you without an income to cover your expenses. Instead, you should start looking for a new job while still employed. This way, you ensure that you have a source of income until you secure a new position.

Additionally, you should assess your financial situation to make sure you have enough savings to cover your expenses during the transition period. It's important to plan for how you'll manage your bills and daily expenses if there is a gap between jobs.

By taking these steps, you're not avoiding risk altogether, but rather making sure the risk you take is manageable and won't leave you in a difficult situation. This approach allows you to pursue new opportunities while minimizing potential negative impacts.

I've seen people from India, starting with nothing, move to different countries with a clear vision of their goals.

Upon arriving in places like America, within a decade or so, they achieve many things they never imagined possible. Many of them lacked formal education, networks, or connections. However, they boldly seized opportunities and stuck to their mantra of 'success.' They focused solely on the possibilities ahead, ignoring any obstacles in their path.

When I was writing my book, I understood how important it is to delegate tasks. At times, I assigned the typing job to my then 11-year-old daughter, Noura. She enthusiastically took my diary and typed several pages for me, aiming to assist her mother.

When you're involved in business or pursuing big goals, there's a lot on your plate. Thinking to do everything alone will slow down your progress. You could even lose your place in the market. That's why it's crucial to have a system and a team supporting you. With a well-functioning system in place, you can earn money even while you sleep! Do you agree?

- With a clear mind, they know how to delegate things to the experts, with the best of the best people in the industry.

When Sensei gave me a big project to edit his leadership book, named, (Sleeper to Leader; Everything you need to know to become an influential leader in any situation) first he asked me about my situation, and whether I could handle it or not. Then, he asked if I was free to take responsibility.

He added it is not an easy task. Out of 184 pages, I am going to give you 13 pages, just go through this.

He told me not to take it as an obligation, to take it only if I have time and passion. Then he sent me 13 pages. He liked the way I edited and drafted. He told me, now I am going to hand over the entire manuscript to you.

He told me to consider it as my book, and whatever changes you make, just mention it. This is your book. This is your responsibility. Then he never bothered about it.

His approach was to empower me to take charge of the work, believing that my commitment would yield amazing results. Despite taking a month-long vacation where I carried the entire manuscript with me to India, both in hard and soft copy, I found it challenging to focus on the task.

When I mentioned this to him, he reassured me, saying there was no need to rush and to take my time. Once I returned from my homeland, I approached the task calmly and without haste. Eventually, I completed the editing.

One fine morning, after a few months I sent him the edited version along with a note of gratitude for trusting me with the project. He expressed his joy and shared that during his morning ritual and prayers, he had remembered the task. It felt like telepathy.

One thing I am particularly grateful for him was that the same day he remembered about the task, even though he had given me many months before. After that, he handed over another book, titled 21 Secrets to Success, Greatness, Happiness & Richness, for review and discussion, including my colleague in the process. This book is now available for readers seeking actionable insights on personal growth and clarity. I thoroughly enjoyed reading it multiple times.

This is just an example of the humble and empathetic approach of people with diamond clarity.

- People with clarity learn how to get out of their way. They learn how to delegate as they grow. All successful people are very good at the art of delegation.

Clarity helps us to seek help whenever needed. People with clarity have mentors and coaches and they have mastermind groups.

What is masterminding? Nowadays, advertisements about masterminding seem to be everywhere online.

Masterminding involves a group of like-minded people up to ten people sitting together to brainstorm ideas, with the belief that multiple brains working together generate more ideas and solutions than one person alone.

During these sessions, one person sits in the hot seat to present their personal or professional challenges, and the group collaborates until solutions are found.

My coach helped in all my ways and is always a call away. That makes a tremendous impact on my life. This book is also the result of his encouragement. During the initial stages of my leadership journey, he trusted me, and assigned a few tasks to me, like giving feedback to my fellow leaders, for their speeches, being their guide to complete the tasks on time, quote master for a quote competition within the community and many more. Which gave me a lot of confidence, courage, and happiness to move forward.

He encourages masterminding. With that, we got a lot of clarity in our challenges, by taking actionable steps. Two brains are better than one. We did it virtually, as we all are in different time zones.

- People with clarity enjoy a fulfilled life. They always dream big. Enjoy the little things of life, and they also help you to lead a clarity-filled life. Their intentions are so clear. They know that the greatest responsibility arises from breakdowns. Clarity guides you to paths you never imagined. Daily reflection is the key to achieving massive results.

Do things that matter. Like sitting by the ocean or going for a walk with your spouse, or making sand castles with your children. My children always invite me to play 'Truth or dare' and 'Would you rather?'. One day I asked my son, if your toys could speak and play with you what would you do?

He said, I will play 'Truth or dare' and 'Would you rather?'. From his words, I understood that this is what he wants. So let us make the world, by balancing the journey called life.

John Assaraf says clarity is the first law of mind. I love that thought, and it is true. Let us keep that in mind.

## Call to Action

Out of all the qualities described, which one resonates with you the most, and how can you begin incorporating it into your life starting today?

CHAPTER 15

# 21 WAYS TO IMPROVE MENTAL CLARITY

*"Mental clarity is the child of courage, not the other way around."*

**– Nassim Nicholas Taleb, a renowned author, statistician, and risk analyst**

John Assaraf suggests that our brain is not merely an organ, but an organism deserving of care and nurturing. Just as we would care for a baby or a beloved pet, we must provide our brains with nourishing thoughts and ample rest. This can involve indulging in positive thinking, trusting yourself in the best way possible, giving yourself applause for what you have already achieved, and taking short breaks to relax, such as enjoying a refreshing cold shower to invigorate your mental muscles.

Have you ever noticed how pets instinctively care for you in the best possible way? Similarly, your brain acts as your protector, signaling potential dangers and urging you to reconsider your actions. It may send signals like, hi, don't start, this may be scary! However, it's important to recognize when these signals are unfounded and to focus on your purpose instead.

By following these steps to nurture your "inner child" and achieve clarity, you can experience heightened productivity and growth in all aspects of life. Let us look at ways to improve mental clarity.

1. **Create a Quiet Space**

   To self-reflect or audit your current situation, (mentally, physically, spiritually, and emotionally) an unavoidable factor you need is a quiet space. Identify those buzzing thoughts; not just a few, right? Too many. In no time, you might find yourself traveling from one continent to another, through countless events, people, and experiences. Give it careful consideration. Whatever is needed, hold on to it; the rest is just weeds, let's cast them into the deep ocean.

   When it comes to your work, find a quiet environment to focus or unwind, minimizing distractions. Decluttering both your mental and physical space can enhance productivity.

   Identifying areas where you feel stuck, and understanding the reasons behind it. *Journal* your thoughts and feelings to clear your mental clutter and gain insights.

2. **Practice Mindfulness and Affirmation.**

   I am practicing John Assaraf's Innercise. This is a series of bursts, meditation, and affirmation, to improve the brain muscles. It helps me a lot in my professional and personal journey to keep calm, to organize my physical space and mental state to prepare my day and close my day.

3. **Create a Daily Routine**

   This means scheduling:

   - A morning routine that preps you mentally and physically for the day ahead.
   - A work schedule is determined by your peak productivity hours or your company's designated time.

- An evening walk, or stretch that makes sure you're not sitting in a chair all day.
- *Plan your day the night before*

4. **List Your Priorities**

   Start doing things by prioritizing. Making your priorities happen comes with mindful planning. Write down a list of things for the next day, and lay out your workout clothes and gear where you'll see them. Prep the ingredients for your meals, and make sure you get enough sleep so you feel rested enough to do it all.

   Benjamin Franklin says "If you fail to plan, you are planning to fail!"

5. **Exercise and Eat a Healthy Diet**

   Just like the rest of your body, your brain thrives on regular movement and the right food.

   Make sure to incorporate a well-rounded diet featuring leafy greens, fatty fish, berries, and walnuts. Additionally, aim for at least two hours of moderate-intensity exercise each week, such as brisk walking, swimming, stair climbing, tennis, or dancing, as these activities are known to support brain health. Don't overlook the importance of staying hydrated by drinking water regularly throughout the day.

6. **Control Your Emotions**

   Regular checking on your emotions and being aware of your feelings help you get clarity, especially when you are in your anger, do not respond, until 24 hours. Emotions are often influenced by your thoughts and perceptions. The way you interpret and think about events and situations can shape your emotional responses to them.

7. **Set Clear Goals**
   Define specific, realistic, and achievable goals. Refer to Part II for details.
8. **Create a Vision Board**
   Visualizing aspirations can be powerful. Suggest creating a vision board with images and words that represent your goals and desires. This will give you momentum.
9. **Take Massive Action**
   Minimize overthinking, as a person of clarity, you know that generalization by writing down will reduce anxiety about getting things done, rather than procrastinating for tomorrow.
10. **Avoid Multitasking**
    Never think about a perfect time to complete a task or never think of a perfect outcome. You become better at something once you practice perfectly in a consistent way. Do commit to yourself.
    Sometimes, you can't think your way to a solution, and the only way to figure out what to do is to just keep 'doing'. Ask 'what if' questions, in a very positive way.
11. **Take Mental Breaks**
    This will give you a boost. Taking a break can enhance productivity and creativity by allowing your mind to rest and rejuvenate. It also helps reduce stress, improving overall mental and physical well-being.
12. **Explore New Hobbies**
    Involvement in new activities or hobbies. Exploring different interests can provide a fresh perspective and ignite passion. Refer to the chapter on how to find out your passion for more details.

13. **Challenge Comfort Zones**
    Encourage stepping out of comfort zones. Once you identify by reflecting on the area you got stuck, shake it off your comfort zone.
14. **Seek Inspiration**
    Recommend books, podcasts, or talks that offer inspiration and guidance. Learning from others who have overcome similar challenges can be motivating.
15. **Network and Connect**
    Building connections with leaders who are better than you, can provide support and open up opportunities. Networking can lead to new ideas and perspectives. Be part of a leadership tribe and sharpen your skills and mindset.
16. **Identify the following Patterns, Fears, Frustrations, and Blame.** Identify any fears that may be holding you back, such as fear of judgment, failure, success, or societal opinions. Uncovering these fears can help you understand their hold on you.

    *Identify frustrations* and prioritize mental and emotional well-being by eliminating unnecessary burdens. Reflecting on past decisions, understanding their consequences, learning from them, and being intentional about designing your friendships, personal growth, and overall life can also help.

    *Recognize that blaming:* Recognize external factors such as parents, schools, or managers may blame or shame you. Listen with awareness and reflect; some feedback may help you grow. If it doesn't align with your truth, let it go and move forward with clarity. Take control and responsibility for your own life.

Personal accountability is essential in examining areas of life where accountability is crucial. This includes evaluating your role in various relationships and being disciplined and in charge of your actions.

17. **Acceptance of the Present and letting go of the Past** is a superpower for emotional freedom. This means releasing emotional baggage and pinpointing what bothers you to work on recovering daily while protecting your emotional well-being through conscious choices.
18. **Get Enough Sleep**

    The less sleep you get, the more your memory and ability to focus go out of the window.

    To improve your chances of getting enough deep sleep, start by revisiting the basics:

    - Build a sleep routine by going to bed and waking up at the same time every day.
    - Block out as much noise and light as possible in your bedroom.
    - Learn how to power nap. This is very useful for days when you don't get enough sleep at night.
    - Avoid eating too late at night, and foods that tend to give you heartburn.

    If you're still experiencing sleep disturbances, it's important to seek advice from a medical professional.
19. **Spend Time in Nature**

    This is a great way to get clarity. Listening to birds chirping, and the sounds of the stream or waves will purify your mind. Wole Soyinka, the award-winning writer and recipient of the 1986 Nobel Prize in Literature, said that whenever he experiences writer's block, he turns to nature or goes hunting. I met him at African Literature festival, Sharjah.

20. **Seek Help**
    If you get stuck, seek help from coaches or mentors.
21. **Limit the Time You Spend on Social Media**
    Reduce social media, and don't intake negative news and threats, to have clear thoughts. Remove as many non-essential apps as possible.

### Call to Action

How would you rate your mental clarity on a scale of 1 to 10? Choose any five practices that resonate with your goals. Commit to incorporating these habits into your routine for improved focus. Regularly reassess and refine your approach.

CHAPTER 16

# THE IMPORTANCE OF HAVING A MENTOR AND AN INSPIRING TRIBE

> ***"Define your chief objective to your coach, stay coachable in the game, and if you take action, your coach can ignite the passion within you that drives real fueling your growth."***

Meeting with the 2017 World Champion of Public Speaking, Manoj prompted my decision to get a coach. He visited Dubai for a keynote speech at the Sharjah International Book Fair in 2018. Rasheed, who is a leadership visibility strategist, was handling the event's PR, and communication, thus, my family and I spent some valuable time with him.

During our conversation, he inquired about my interests and suggested to join Toastmasters. Despite my hesitation about waiting until my child turned five years of age, he urged me to start now, assuring me that I could begin by observing the speeches and gradually participating at my own pace for the speaking engagements. I was a homemaker then, taking care of my kids and family.

He added that after joining a club, he started speaking only after nine months and a shy introverted personality then.

Whatever you say, like 'I will join after my son turns 'X' number of years, or once I earn more money, all these are your excuses.

He ensured that we needed a foundation to start our personal development journey. Communities like Toastmasters, speaking clubs, or leadership groups can inspire you to take action, thus you can enjoy the journey towards growth. He inspires me in many ways. He added, join a small club, which will give you a lot of opportunities to take up so that you can build your confidence.

I found my community, team, my unique call, and how to add value to people's lives by finding out my unique strength. He always asks people to find out their unique 'gifts' and find out their 'kingmaker' to shorten their journey.

Because of this conversation, when I got a chance to meet Sensei virtually, I decided to make him my mentor to start my leadership journey early and prepare myself well in advance. So that I can work on my goals, step by step to reach my destination.

Sensei helps in reducing my learning curve, with his decades of research and development of his study materials. He simplified my journey toward success.

That is how I could come up with this book in front of you. His method of 'SPARKER' technique gave me immense clarity in my journey. Now I can bring clarity to others' lives as well, with the wisdom he showered.

When it comes to book writing Manoj influenced me, when I saw, he was sitting and signing his leadership book, hosted by Toastmasters International District 105, which represents the UAE, Oman, Jordan, and Lebanon in the region, leader Manoj addressed the UAE Toastmasters community of nearly 3,000 members at this event in Dubai. The interactive session, titled "Ask Manoj Anything", was held at the Emirates Headquarters

Auditorium in Dubai in 2017. This event made Rasheed receiving a special PR award from Toastmasters District 127.

I attended that session with great enthusiasm. However, I couldn't sit in the front row and listen attentively because I had my infant cradled along with a 5-year-old daughter.

Knowing he wouldn't stay quiet for long in a crowded room and might cry or make noise, I watched the show from near the back door of the hall, away from everyone so that nobody would be disturbed, the hall was so large that I could barely see the stage from that distance, however, I managed to listen to his speech.

Inspired by this show, I started thinking seriously about writing a book, although this thought has been there since 2009.

He gave me an idea, by showcasing himself as a model. I visualized myself in that seat. Sensei hold me accountable to reach there and encouraged me to write more by repeatedly saying that writing and editing are my major strengths.

I still remember an incident from my college days. While reading literature with friends, the teacher asked us to read together to practice empathy, considering both fast and slow readers. However, the fast readers became irritated, as they lost the reading flow while waiting for others to complete each page. During this reading session, I turned to my accountability partner and said, "Hi, I know I can express these thoughts better in writing." She stared at me in wonder and smiled at me. That smile made my day because it served as a source of inspiration for me. I always remember that smile, whenever I write something. I considered it a positive acknowledgment, and she shared that with my other classmates.

Now, coming back to mentoring, I can tell you that a mentor or coach can shorten your journey toward greatness. You don't have to do it all by yourself. It will take time. If you have a coach or mentor, they will give you constructive feedback. They will guide you in creating your road map, and guide you in implementing feedback. Keep you motivated, and be there to check on you. In your silence, they will be there to ask you what happened. It happened in my life many times. Stay coachable

Even the president of a country or head of a state has coaches in different areas of their lives. Without coaches or mentors, you will be wasting years.

My mentor and fellow members of the community are there to support and motivate me to do more. A lot of my clients have reported that they were able to accomplish significant goals in their lives following the coaching sessions.

They can suggest to you people with similar goals, who already achieved the same goal. It can boost your confidence; you get more opportunities. Always go for the best of the best. Find out the right person to take you to the next level. A mentor will never take credit when you achieve something.

Being coachable is crucial to becoming a champion. Your coach can identify your blind spots and strengths.

Earlier, I didn't have a coach. So, my dreams became mere dreams, without any timeline. Back in 2009, when I reached the Middle East, I started visiting different kinds of Expos, with interesting agendas, the world's largest book fair, which was conducted every year in September, and many more. I found many of my friends, and Rasheed's friends and teachers whom I met here are keen on publishing books. Rasheed is assisting numerous individuals in publishing their books and gaining visibility in their respective fields. He even worked as a ghostwriter during his college days to earn pocket money for his studies.

Now, I am also part of that journey, guiding others to structure their thoughts persuasively.

I too believed I needed to write about many things. At first, the topics that came to mind were writing about my recipes, then gardening, and later coaching, but my focus kept shifting. I began writing quotes with the goal of publishing a book after completing 100 quotes.

Then by reflecting on being my own coach, I got a spark, to write about coaching. Because this is what I do, clarity coaching. And this is what I wanted to learn and practice. What I am passionate about and what I enjoy the most should be shared through my writing to empower others to find their call.

Until I found Sensei, I lacked clarity on how to start writing, even though I published a few of my articles in the newspaper.

Finding a coach in the writing field can potentially increase your return on investment by providing guidance, feedback, and strategies to improve your writing skills and marketability, ultimately leading to greater success and recognition in the industry. Return on investment in writing refers to the benefits or gains achieved from the time, effort, and resources invested into writing activities.

My belief is that if you want to become something, you should learn from those who have already achieved it and experienced it. For example, if your goal is to become a New York Times bestseller, learn from someone who has reached that milestone.

Their experience will offer far more valuable insights than someone who has only written books but hasn't achieved that level of success. Whatever your goal may be, seek out the experts who have already walked that path.

Rasheed asked me to write 100 words every day, however, there was no timeline. No strategy. I didn't know consistency matters. During the pandemic, I attended book-writing workshops. I became part of many book-launching ceremonies at the world's largest book fair. Though all these gave me an instant boost, nothing worked well until I met my mentor.

In 2023, my close friend came from India, who is a senator, and academician at a prestigious university in Kerala, came to Sharjah, to release her translation of a book, which again inspired me to release my book soon.

I plan to debut my book at the Sharjah International Book Fair in 2024. It is one of the world's largest book fairs, and it has over 400 literary events. Before that during Manoj's next visit, to the UAE in 2024 he invited me to speak about my book on his stage, even though he had a lot of content to share.

So what I am saying is that a coach can shorten your journey toward greatness. They will give you their time, in return respect their words and time. Follow their discipline and habits. Go for the best of the best coaches or mentors.

My mentor always asks, "If you have chest pain, whom will you approach, a general practitioner or a cardiologist?" Until I met him, I was visiting all the general practitioners, and learning different things. Now I have clarity on whom I should approach. It must be an expert.

Anyone who wishes for growth needs to seek help, from coaches, mentors, consultants, or community members. Each one of us requires mentoring, guidance, and counsel to get better clarity on our vision, passions, goals, and life in general.

**Call to Action**

Do you have a mentor? If you could see yourself ten years from now, what kind of mentor would your future self say you needed today to unlock the greatest version of who you are destined to become?

CHAPTER 17

# THE CLARITY WHEEL

---

*"It is during our darkest moments that we must focus to see the light."*

**– Aristotle Onassis,**
**Greek shipping industrialist**

---

The Clarity Wheel is a tool that helps you understand how to distribute your time, focus, and energy, and identify the areas where you need to set meaningful goals. Most of us can focus heavily on one or a few areas. The issue with that is that you leave the other areas unattended. When you do that, you miss out on important areas of life. It's like driving a vehicle with only three wheels instead of four, unstable and difficult to move forward. Life works the same way. To experience true peace and ease, all areas must be attended to and balanced.

It is a tool that helps people check how different areas of their lives are going and make adjustments to find a good balance and happiness.

Imagine life as a big, colorful wheel with different sections, just like a rainbow. Each part of the wheel is like a piece of your life, such as your career, learning, being with family, and staying healthy. The wheel helps you see if everything is balanced and you are leading a happy life. If one part needs more attention, you can spin the wheel and make it better.

As you look at the wheel, identify the areas where you're strong and those that have received the least attention or consideration. Here is where you need to start paying attention.

This is a crucial part of your Next-level life events and getting you an action plan for your strongest life. I have seen people who live in the metropolitan area, they work, work, and work, forget to take care of their health, by not knowing what they put into their mouth, or the timing of their food, and forget to take a break from the busy hours and sleep early and wake up early. Thus, in their thirties, and forties, they die of heart attack or fall into chronic illness.

**Now let us Have a Look at the Areas in the Clarity Wheel:**

a) Business,
b) Career/work
c) Relationship
d) Wealth/Finance
e) Health and Fitness/Wellness
f) Personal Growth and Development
g) Contribution
h) Spirituality (Spiritual development and inner peace)
i) Personal environment
j) Fun and recreation

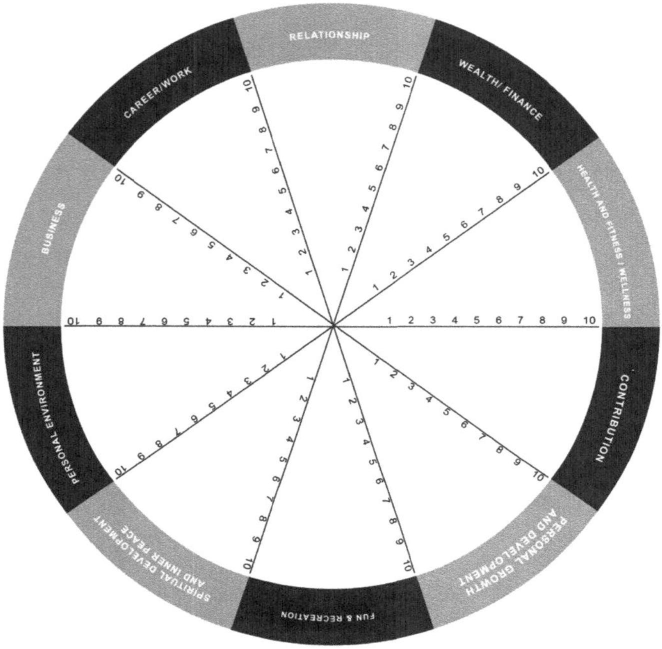


The clarity wheel is a great starting place for you to create a balance, to bring clarity to your life. You can bring a lot of joy and happiness, once you start working on these spokes. The purpose of the clarity wheel is to identify how satisfied you are with your current life and how you can lead a joyful life.

Draw a dot between the centre of the circle and the outer circle to represent the amount you feel fulfilled in the area, with the centre representing zero percent and the outer edge representing 100 percent.

There is no right or wrong numbering. The number first comes to your mind would be your reality, no need to scratch your head. Whatever number you put, must inspire you to take action.

What I did, when I was doing this task was if I want to rate six for my career, I purposefully rate five, so that I could take extra care of that area, and I did the same for all the wheels.

Once you draw a dot in each column according to your life and how much you feel fulfilled, connect the dots together to make a web. That is your life now. Now the remaining part outside of the web which is in white is the part where you need to focus.

Let us explain a little more to understand the concept. Once you start acting on it, consider one area to focus on.

For example, if you take 'relationship', go back to your drawing board, and write down the score you got in your 'clarity journal'. Then out of 'relationship' you take one single dot, which is your relationship with your teammates.

Then identify all the strengths and weaknesses, the patterns you have, when you interact with them. Write everything down. Ask yourself, does your relationship with your teammates give you happiness?

Understand the things that you want to change, you want to improve, etc. It will not happen overnight.

It is all about polishing your character and behavior. I believe you got it. Then once you start identifying your nature, start aligning with your values all the time you are in touch with your team. Intentionally speak, listen, respond, and act.

Once you start practicing this, your relationship with all the connections may start improving. Likewise based on your pace, you need to focus on all the areas, slowly. Remember, you can't eat an elephant in one bite!

If you take the personal development area, ask yourself, how committed are you to empowering yourself? Are you satisfied with the direction you are going?

If you take fun and recreation, ask yourself, do you have activities that help you enjoy life or activities that recharge you?

In all areas, you can create some questions, based on your thoughts and ideas.

# Ask yourself, how do you feel, a particular area. You don't have to be 100 percent in any of the areas, because human beings are not perfect. You can aim to be a peak performer. If you are a peak performer, there are still chances for improvement. Focus on one degree change every day in your life, it could be a small move. This is life. It is all about daily improvement and growth.

# Ask yourself, what do you want to do in the next 30 days to increase your fulfillment and joy?

After 6 months redraw your wheel of clarity, or take a printout from this page, and rework, re-evaluate, and adjust your actions according to the rating. You see the variation in your graph. Growth happens gradually.

### Call to Action

Which is your strong area, and which area needs reinforcement? Write down.

# CHAPTER 18

# THE LEGACY

---

*"As a writer, and so my legacy is writings. As far as I am concerned, I consider my books my legacy, and not an institution"*

**– Peter Drucker,**
**Management consultant, educator, and author**

---

I could connect with the above wisdom of Peter Drucker, the big thinker. My legacy is my writings, coaching and teaching. I share my thoughts through my words, and I believe they are going to be used by future generations even a hundred years from now.

I followed in the footsteps of my paternal grandparents, who were teachers in a specialized field. My grandmother's mother was also a teacher. I emulate their approach and resilience in confronting the toughest situations.

The common thing I saw in them is they were peaceful and they could connect with people very easily. They were accepted by people around them in their thoughts, and they were available to their people.

As we are sent down to this planet, we need to ask self-reflective questions about ourselves and about our true existence. I have asked this, during my leadership journey, and I got stuck. I had no answer for many months. I got confused about many answers I got for this.

Have you ever asked yourself, "What do I want to be remembered for?" It is a question that induces you to renew yourself because it pushes you to see yourself as a different person, the person you want to be. You need to focus away from yourself towards the contribution you would like to make in the lives of others.

As human beings, you and I will eventually depart from this world, leaving behind valuable contributions for future generations. Therefore, I cannot conclude this book without emphasizing the importance of clarity in leaving a legacy.

Create memories with others and ensure that long before we depart, you have made significant contributions for the benefit of future generations.

In order to create the legacy you truly want, start building your team years in advance. Empower them to lead with responsibility and reflection. When your values are lived consistently, not just spoken, they shape others silently. True followers observe not only your words, but your stillness, your decisions, your discipline, your intent. And when those observations turn into aligned actions, legacy doesn't just survive, it multiplies across generations."

When my clients come to me seeking solutions for procrastination, I pose one crucial question: "What will people say about you when you're gone?" This question prompts them to reflect deeply and discover their core values, urging them to live in alignment with their purpose. Which gives them a sense of urgency to act on their purpose. As a result, they realize the importance of structuring their lives according to their values and living intentionally.

When I read the magazine "The Super Hundred," a collection of inspirational life stories of entrepreneurs, professionals, and corporate houses from India, based in the Middle East and Africa, I noticed that all 100 leaders were discussing their legacy. Truly inspirational. I am so happy to see one of the members of my leadership community, shared his legacy stories in this, who is Zaindheen PB, Group Director of Dubai-based industrial major Hotpack Global.

Legacy is the story of your life that lives on after you leave this earth. Legacy is crafted by our faithful everyday choices. Anyone can truly leave a lasting legacy, on one condition: live each moment purposefully or intentionally, knowing that time is the greatest equalizer everyone has, and it needs to be handled consciously. When I met my mentor in Dubai, he spoke passionately about his various programs and collaborations. Of them all, the one he valued most was his 52-week leadership course, designed to build legacy leaders who would carry these lessons forward and teach them for years to come.

### Call to Action

What contributions do you want to leave behind as your legacy? How does the story of your life change the world for generations to come?

Write it down in your 'CJ'. Keep it in a place where your family can read it and join you in leading a fulfilled and inspiring life. Take a moment to reflect on the impact you aspire to make on the lives of others and consider what actions you can take today to begin building that legacy.

# PART II

# LET US PIECE THE PUZZLE TOGETHER!

*"The impossible cannot be where there is perseverance and faith. There is no impossible in life."*

**– His Highness Sheikh Mohammed bin Rashid Al Maktoum, Vice President and Prime Minister of the United Arab Emirates (UAE) and the Ruler of Dubai.**

## Introduction

Welcome to **"Let's Piece the Puzzle Together"**, a focused segment on the leadership discipline of goal setting, your framework for overcoming challenges, breaking barriers, and achieving meaningful progress. Just like fitting together puzzle pieces reveals a beautiful picture, this part of the book is all about assembling the elements of your life (health, wealth, relationship, career, personal investment, spirituality, contribution, etc.) to create something incredible.

Get ready to embark on a journey where you will explore the puzzle of your life and set goals that align with your dreams. It's time to unlock your potential and craft a masterpiece of fulfillment and success.

Throughout this part, you would beguided through mastering your dream life. First, it is essential to take full responsibility for your actions with a hundred percent commitment and an abundance mindset, to set and achieve goals you desire to achieve. Just focus on you, and where are you right now emotionally, mentally, spiritually, and intellectually or skill-wise, and walk forward. Focus and follow what your intuition says to you.

Success begins with taking intentional, massive action toward your goals. Embrace ownership of your tasks and learn from your mistakes. Dare to infuse your journey with love and laughter, they fuel resilience.

> ***And remember, passion is the soul of progress; it turns your goals into a mission worth pursuing. Take inspired action every single day toward your goals and dreams.***

Close your eyes for a moment and think about the benefits you can enjoy once you start living purposefully by having compelling goals and visions for your personal and professional life. Find more reasons for your existence. Write down those in your 'CJ'

Download all the chaos from your mind by practicing clarity and take wise action toward your wildest goals. Let the puzzling adventure begin!

Can you see the life you want to live, the property you would love to buy, the charity you are supporting, or the other vivid pictures in your mind right now?

CHAPTER 19

# FROM CHAOS TO CLARITY: THE SECRET TO HITTING YOUR GOALS

*"The more clarity you have, the easier it is to focus. And when you focus, you achieve."*

**– Tony Robbins,**
**life coach and author**

Life is a sacred expedition, I believe you and I are all part of. Every scripture, every inspirational voice talks about one thing, how to live a fulfilled life. The answer lies in giving utmost care to the life we got.

It means making wise decisions based on what the heart says, not just what the moment demands. It means living with enthusiasm, having courage to face challenges, and setting strong goals. Not just any goals, but intentional ones, backed by deliberate thoughts and consistent action.

To lead a goal-oriented life, you and I need clarity. We must know how to manage our minutes, hours, days, weeks, months, and years wisely. Time doesn't wait. It keeps moving forward, and so must we. Without clarity, time disappears unnoticed, and we are left wondering where it all went.

Each day, we're given the same 24 hours. The one resource equally distributed to all, regardless of who we are or where we come from. What sets us apart is how purposefully we choose to use it. To use time wisely, we must take deliberate action. And to act with intent, we must have clear goals. Without direction, even the most abundant time slips through unnoticed. The real question isn't how much time we have, it's what we do with it.

As we discussed in the first part, to lead a meaningful life, we must first understand why we are here on this earth. Goal setting is a deeply meaningful exercise. It is not just about writing down ambitions; it is about crafting a vision for your future. It gives you a sense of direction, guiding you on what to do, where to focus your energy, and in which direction you need to move. Without goals, life becomes a series of random events. With goals, every moment holds purpose, and every step takes us closer to the life we aspire to create.

Goal achievement doesn't just end with personal satisfaction, it becomes a beacon of visibility. People start to notice your commitment, consistency, and success. That recognition creates more room for you to contribute your talents, connect with new audiences, and scale your impact. In today's world, success often speaks louder than words, and goals are the megaphone.

## From Cradle to Conquest: Navigating Life's Milestones

From the very first day of your life, you have had goals, whether they were conscious or innate instincts guiding you. Take a moment to reflect on them and see where they lead you.

From day one, you instinctively search for your mother's bosom, looking around to identify family members. Your initial goals include crying and basic movements. Over time, these evolve into milestones, such as smiling to others, responding to colors, grabbing toys, and more.

As you grow, your goals change, and you navigate life until eventually, you depart from this world. From infancy, curiosity drives you to experiment, from lying down to walking. Despite warnings from the adults, you persist, learning, and achieving.

Just as you didn't stop exploring as infants, embracing curiosity and dedication fuels your accomplishments. Day by day, your goals are changing. You started from an infant to a grown-up man or woman, living your life, and must once leave this planet. Embrace this growth with clarity and purpose, for it is the essence of your existence.

The example above illustrates that every day, whether consciously or unconsciously, you have goals. During infancy, you are driven by strong goals and a curiosity to explore.

From simple actions like lying on the bed to milestones like crawling, sitting, and walking, you constantly strive to achieve.

You start doing, experimenting with things, fall or fail, again standing up, by closing ears to many 'no's, focusing, giving up, you may feel stressed, still moving on, by achieving something, failing miserably! However, you must stand and face the challenges. This is the right way to achieve your goals.

This reflects the essence of goal-setting in your journey through life, it demands purpose, intention, and clarity about your desires and aspirations.

Setting goals is a process that changes over time. The goals you set in your twenties will most likely be very different from those goals you set in your forties. There is a clear difference between the goals set by a high school student and those set by a college student. No one has ever become a successful person by simply sitting on the couch.

Goal setting is also like that! You need to be purposeful; you need to be intentional. When no one gives you a hand, the clarity call will, and that moment will become your breakthrough. When you make the call , you begin to show up as your most powerful, focused, and authentic version. Nothing will bother you, other than what your intuition says.

Your unsure self will meet a rushing soul, eager to rise, and from that union, the clarity beast will be born. Here you stop chasing everything, and start building something. That's when average turns into extraordinary, not overnight, but with intention, clarity, focus, and truth.

### Call to Action

Reflect on your past goals and experiences. Did you fulfill those goals? What happened to them? Write down five challenges you faced during the journey and the feelings you have experienced upon accomplishing them.

CHAPTER 20

# UNSTOPPABLE GOALS: TURN DREAMS INTO REALITY

Goals encompass everything you want to accomplish, experience, or see in life, and they can be tangible or intangible. Tangible goals are measurable, like running a five-K marathon, or saving $10,000 per month etc.

Intangible goals focus on personal growth, or personal investments, such as improving patience or becoming a better listener, or healing a relationship. These are harder to measure, they enrich your overall well-being.

## Unshakeable Identity: Owning Your Uniqueness

### Why are Goals Unique?

Each individual's goals are unique and meaningful. You are one of a kind because your mind works in a way no one else's does. An unrepeatable life algorithm shaped by your journey, beliefs, and choices. The way you think, feel, and move through the world creates an energy that only you can bring. Your thoughts, timing, and emotions are like a fingerprint. No one can replicate them and that is what makes you powerful.

The environment you live in, the upbringing you have, the surroundings, everything is different from person to person. Moreover, your dreams are different from those of the other person. Where do you stand right now, mentally, spiritually, and emotionally is different from other people?

Your goals draw you in, helping you prioritize what truly matters and eliminate distractions. You must know what are the things you want to achieve in your life. It could be:

- Healing an important relationship.
- Achieving a big health goal, (it could be getting eight hours of sleep every day, for the next three months or longer, to improve your overall health and energy levels).
- Conducting a webinar on your topic of interest.
- Getting a new job in your passionate area.
- Getting out of debt, creating an emergency fund for yourself and your family.
- Producing a movie.
- Create your podcast series.
- Changing career.
- Getting a promotion, or pay raise.
- Working toward your legacy, or what?

The possibilities are endless, as there are millions of people on this planet Earth with millions of choices. Take a moment to grab a pen and 'CJ', and start jotting down your goals, even the ones that may seem hidden deep within you, waiting to be discovered.

In a rapidly changing world, it's essential to ask yourself: Are you living simply, or are you actively engaged in adapting to the evolving landscape? Consider what you're doing with this precious gift of life bestowed upon us by the creator or the great universal power. Asking empowering questions will give you clarity on what you want to achieve. Rather than asking superficial questions, since we are focusing on gaining clarity in life, ask self-reflective, deeper-level questions to ensure that, without excuses, you commit to living fully. The results will be massive, from inspiring those around you and people across the globe and thus leading a truly joyful life.

## Let your Goals Drive You Because You are Still Breathing

You and I need to understand the value of life and why it's crucial to lead an intentional life. The most precious gift in our life is that we are still breathing. Before it ends, we need to do a lot for ourselves and a lot for others. This is where the importance of goals, vision, purpose, and passion comes in. Every day, discover what excites you, as it will offer valuable clues about where you should focus your energy.

It's not about what others are doing or what their goals are. your life is solely yours. It is meant for you. Time is ticking, and no matter how the result unfolds, what matters is how intentionally you live each day. Was it joyous? Create your own chapters.

When I read Henry David Thoreau's Walden, I came across this powerful statement: 'If one advances confidently in the direction of his dreams, and endeavors to live the life which he has imagined, he will meet with a success unexpected in common hours."

It means that by confidently pursuing your dreams and living intentionally, you will achieve success in ways you never expected.

As a person seeking clarity, it's essential to take time to define 'who you are'. Individuals often define themselves in various ways:

- By emotions, such as "I am a lover"
- By positions, like "I am a CEO"

- By professions, like "I am a teacher"
- By roles, like "I am editor-in-chief"
- By behaviors, such as "I am a drunkard"
- By possessions, like "I am a property·owner"
- By others' feedback, like "I am not worthy enough"
- By spiritual beliefs, such as "I am Jew," and so forth.

To gain a deeper understanding of yourself, find a quiet, relaxed space for reflection. Allow your mind to be curious and refrain from judgment. Consider journaling with open-ended questions to facilitate this process.

**Call to Action**

Write down the insights you discover; remember, these perceptions may evolve over time, and you can refine them as you grow. Crafting thoughtful responses will guide you toward your desired destination. Afterward, review your reflections. Are you content with them?

CHAPTER 21

# CLARITY IN GOAL SETTING

*"If you set goals and go after them with all the determination you can muster, your gifts will take you places that will amaze you."*

**– Les Brown**

**World's No.1 motivational speaker**

Have you ever set an exciting, personal goal that has moved you forward, not to impress others but to fulfill yourself? What happened to that goal? Did you achieve it, or did it fade away after a month or so?

If you don't have a single goal yet, and you are living a life on autopilot, don't worry, you're not alone. Almost every one of us has goals. Like me, I had beautiful goals without a system, strategy, or timeline.

You might wait for a magic wand or divine moment, however, that is not a reliable strategy.

Setting goals is as simple as putting pen to paper and following a systematic approach, strategy, and focus. You can turn your dreams into reality with the right mindset, commitment, and inspired action.

Be clear first on your most important objective. You need to gain deeper clarity around your purpose to know the importance of your goals. You should have clarity on Where you are heading?, the emotions you want to experience, the lifestyle you want to live, the health you want to maintain, including your ideal BMI, and the kind of person you want to become. To ground this concept, refer back to the earlier section on clarity.

To reflect on these, you need to know what are the things you don't want to focus in your life, what are the things you need to change in your life, what are the things you need to stop, what are the thoughts you need to eliminate, what are the behaviors you need to take care of, what are the habits and routines you need to work on, what is the mindset you need to cultivate, what are the skills you need to develop, what is the training you need to enroll in, where do you focus more, and how you are draining or utilising your energy. And you may add more.

### The Determined Salmon: A Lesson on Focus and Clarity

Let us learn from the salmon. Every year, thousands of salmon swim upstream against fierce currents and numerous obstacles, driven by an innate clarity of purpose: to return to the very spot where they were born and lay their eggs. It's a risky journey, raging waters, predators, and even their own physical limitations.

Yet, despite the odds, these salmon are unyielding. They swim tirelessly toward their goal, knowing exactly where they need to go. Their bodies may tire, their strength may wane, but their focus remains fixed.

This natural instinct mirrors the power of clarity in our own lives. Just as the salmon knows its goal and follows its path with unwavering determination, we too need clarity of purpose. It's not about avoiding obstacles, however, about staying focused on what truly matters, even when the journey gets tough. The salmon doesn't waste energy on distractions; it knows its end goal is worth the struggle.

When you are clear about your purpose, you become like the salmon, resilient and determined, navigating through challenges with conviction, knowing that the effort will lead to something greater.

Clarity is the first law of the mind, John Assaraf says.

John Maxwell says, "Clarity comes before strategy"

> **"*Goal setting starts with deciding what you want to achieve. By taking consistent steps and checking your progress, you can eventually experience the freedom of reaching your dreams.*"**

You can set goals in different areas of your life. Kindly refer back the chapter 'The Clarity Wheel'

## Selection of Goals

Goals can be large and challenging goals, or smaller and more personal. It all depends on what you want to achieve, and what deadline you have in mind.

Let us start small. List up to 3 goals that you are currently pursuing. These can be small or large goals, anything that you are aiming to accomplish. Whether it is small or large, you need to use the power of imagination. Your imagination helps you to think without a ceiling. Forget about your limitations. Your mind can bring the most creative ideas. Grab your 'CJ' and a pen or pencil. Write it down, before it leaves you.

Now coming back to the selection of goals, how to select goals? Write the most important goal that come to your mind, in 30 minutes. They say that if you can't express your goal in 45 seconds to a minute, it's not a goal, it's just a dream. When you have clarity, you can articulate your vision concisely, making it easier to take action and turn your dreams into reality. Tony Robbins emphasizes the importance of actionable plans, stating, "If you talk about it, it's a dream; if you envision it, it's possible; but if you schedule it, it's real."

Now don't give importance to where you are right now, based on money, skill, or knowledge. Just put it in your paper. Now focus on Writing 50 goals that you want to accomplish in your life.

Once you have your list, ask yourself how many years you want to take, to achieve these goals. Categorize them as 1, 3, 5, 10-year goals. Now take 4 from each category, based on your priority. You will have 16 goals in total.

| **1-year goal** | **3-year goal** | **5-year goal** | **10-year goal** |
|---|---|---|---|
| 1 | 1 | 1 | 1 |
| 2 | 2 | 2 | 2 |
| 3 | 3 | 3 | 3 |
| 4 | 4 | 4 | 4 |

Now start working on it. You need to divide the short-term goals into small chunks. Commit yourself to completing the small tasks to reach your goals, thus you work on your long-term goals as well. Start now! Break your short-term goals into manageable tasks and commit to completing them, fueling your long-term success. Each night, list your tasks for the next day, allowing your subconscious to generate new ideas while you sleep. Check off completed items for momentum, and appreciate your efforts, energize yourself!

Every night, list down all the items you must complete the next day. Let us name it the accomplishment list. Allow your subconscious mind to work on the list while you sleep, so you can wake up with new ideas on how to achieve them.

Tick off the items that you have completed, to give you that momentum. Don't forget to appreciate yourself. Do not wait for someone to do that. It is your responsibility to energize yourself.

Ask yourself some clarity questions. What can I, and only I can do that if done well will make a real difference? [This question originated from Peter Drucker.]

CHAPTER 22

# BENEFITS OF GOALS SETTING

*"Each of you, as an individual, must pick your own goals. Listen to others, but do not become a blind follower."*

**– Thurgood Marshall,**
**Civil rights lawyer**

In search of personal and professional growth, goal-setting emerges as a transformative tool, guiding individuals towards purposeful achievements. This chapter explores some benefits of the act of setting goals. Join us on a journey to untie the profound advantages that arise from the intentional pursuit of meaningful objectives.

**Let us Check the Benefits of Goal-setting**

- Goal setting helps you to be clear on what you want and what you don't want. That will give momentum to kick start, whatever the situation may be.
- You will get a clear picture of where you want to reach. As I mentioned, once I completed the discovery coaching with Sensei, I understood my purpose. I understood the need to focus on one target at a time and take strategic action. Have a big plan.

- A plan and a road map are essential to reach where you want to reach. It motivates you. If you have a proper road map, you know your system, what is working well, and what is not working for you.
- Goals make you happy and content because your life is disciplined, and every day you achieve some milestones, which make you happy. This leads to boosted confidence, self-respect, self-esteem, and self-recognition as if you are building your muscle power!
- The goal gives you a starting point. The first step is the hardest, often accompanied by inner chatter telling you to wait, or that you're not capable or worthy. The person who sets a goal creates inspiring words to make it happen and ultimately reaches the finish line. Thus, you can produce results.
- As you focus on your goal, you prioritize your tasks by decluttering your mind. You know how to manage your tasks, eliminating excuses like "I don't have time," "I am not ready yet," "I don't have money to start," "I don't have skills," "I am too old to start," etc. Once you prioritize your tasks, you can track your progress effectively.
- Goals help you become laser-focused, akin to an eagle soaring from a higher altitude, spotting its prey, and seizing it with precision. Let's consider a scenario where distractions lead you astray from your goal, illustrating how this happens in reality.

Have you ever been in a situation, where you come up to YouTube for studies, and end up watching all the other stuff on YouTube one after the other? Finally, you feel so tired, mentally and emotionally, and feel lost and stressed out for not producing results.

- Goals give you energy. It can change your life. Your goals must be purpose-oriented, otherwise, you may lose interest, and you don't know why you are doing what you are doing. Your purpose shouldn't change.

The purpose is primary and your goal is secondary. There is a huge difference between your goal, purpose, vision, and passion.

> ❖ ***Passion is doing what you love.***
> ❖ ***Purpose is your profound "why."***
> ❖ ***Goal is your defined "what."***
> ❖ ***Strategy is your grand "how."***
> ❖ ***Tactics are your crucial milestones.***

Here let me explain the tactics. The remaining points like purpose goal, and strategy we explained earlier. Tactics are the smaller, specific actions or tasks that you undertake to accomplish larger goals or objectives. They are strategic steps that help you make progress toward achieving your overarching goals. Each tactic is designed to contribute to the overall success of your plan by addressing specific aspects or requirements necessary for reaching your desired outcome.

- Goal setting helps you learn the art of saying 'no' when needed. You know it is really hard to say 'no' to others. You must learn this. Because around you there are energy suckers and time suckers. If someone is taking your time, which you allocate for your personal growth or completing a task, you must have the courage to say no, because you need to respect yourself and love yourself.

You must know how to set healthy boundaries. Initially, I believed that setting boundaries was not a good strategy and that I had to put others first. However, once I understood the positive results of setting boundaries, I realized that it is not a crime but rather a part of self-love.

The following story will help you understand how to say no when someone expects you to do more than you are capable of.

When my friend's boss repeatedly asked her to work late, she finally set a boundary by saying, "I would love to help out in the late hours. However, if I do, I won't be productive in the coming days." Initially, her boss was surprised, but he respected her request and adjusted his expectations. As a result, she felt more balanced and productive, proving that setting boundaries can lead to mutual respect and better outcomes.

Be proud of yourself. Congratulate yourself.

> ***Seeking congratulations from others is a sign of immaturity, whereas congratulating yourself is a sign of maturity. You deserve appreciation.***

Create an achievement list. Everyone says 'to-do list'. Instead, let us say 'achievement list'. It is an empathetic approach. To-do list' means it feels like someone is forcing you to do it, instead, if you say achievement list, that gives you some 'aha' feeling, and once you complete each task, review the list you created, and mark off the ones you've achieved with red ink. Then, celebrate your small wins. Take a break. Go out with your friends, kids, or family.

## Call to Action

What benefits have you experienced from setting goals in your life? Take a moment to reflect on how goal-setting has helped you organize your time, track your progress, and stay laser-focused.

CHAPTER 23

# STEPS TO ACHIEVE GOALS

---

*"The path to success is built one bold step at a time: clarity like Bezos, risk like Musk, resilience like Oprah, and vision like Blakely. Millionaires aren't born with maps, they create them through relentless action and uncompromising belief."*

**– Inspired by the journeys of modern-day self-made millionaires**

---

Goals require discipline. Successful people surpass theirs by starting small, building healthy habits, and staying consistent. For motivation, read biographies of successful people. Follow these steps to achieve your goals. This is a tried and tested method I personally follow. To make your goals systematic and achievable, follow these five foundational steps:

1. **Make the Clarity Call to Yourself** 🧘
   Allow uninterrupted time for self-reflection. Awareness is your most powerful tool, it reveals the truth about who you are, where you stand, and what you truly desire.

2. **Identify Your Passion and Purpose**
   Revisit your deepest interests and the reason you feel called to act. As mentioned in the first part, identifying your passion and purpose gives your goals direction and meaning.
3. **Define Your Five Core Values**
   Even in your most difficult moments, your core values will serve as your compass. They shape your decisions, influence your behavior, and keep you grounded.
   People aligned with their core values rarely loses their way.
4. **Acknowledge Your Challenges**
   Be honest about your weaknesses, emotional turbulence, and mental blocks. Recognizing these obstacles is the first step toward overcoming them.
5. **Decide Exactly What You Want**
   Only 10% of people are clear about their desires, financially, for their health, or for their family. Clarity is a superpower that activates your subconscious to help you succeed.
6. **Write it Down**
   Only 3% of people have written goals. Writing activates your mental powers and engages your subconscious.
7. **Make a List**
   List everything that can help you achieve your goal. Break tasks down into manageable steps, like strengthening your financial literacy or starting a meditation practice.
8. **Set Priorities**
   With a plan in place, prioritize your tasks. Ordinary people achieve extraordinary things with a specific and clear plan.
9. **Set a Deadline**
   A deadline signals to your mind that you can't avoid the goal. It motivates you to take action. For long-term goals, break them into smaller tasks or milestones.

10. **Recognize and Develop Your Skills**
    Identify the skills you're confident in and focus on sharpening them. Skill development builds self-assurance and fuels the boldness required to pursue your goals with conviction.
11. **Take Massive Action**
    Consistent action turns dreams into reality. The first step is always the hardest, however, it's essential. Take massive, strategic action, don't settle for average efforts.

Unwritten goals are fantasies. Write your goals in first-person, in running letters, and rewrite them every morning to engage your subconscious fully. Every single night, before going to bed, rather than going to social media, read out your written goals. Repeat this, early morning, either before or after your rituals. In the early hours of your day, avoid social media and scrolling. What you feed your mind in the first few hours of the morning is crucial, as it holds the power to either make or break you. Review as mentioned earlier.

What can you do differently to achieve your goals? What steps can you take today to move closer to achieving them? Write any two steps you would take.

## Goal Clarity Framework

Use this framework to clearly map out your goals, identify possible paths, confront challenges, and recognize the internal patterns that may be influencing your progress. This table serves as a self-reflective tool to enhance clarity and alignment with your personal values.

| Key Goals | Options to Achieve | Current Beliefs / Fears | Challenges/ Threats/ Habits | Solutions/ Action Steps | News Beliefs | Support System / Resources |
|---|---|---|---|---|---|---|
| | | | | | | |
| | | | | | | |
| | | | | | | |
| | | | | | | |
| | | | | | | |

Once you complete these two exercises, the path toward your goals will become clearer. Don't just write them down, print them out and place them somewhere you can see every day. These worksheets are not one-time tasks. They are tools meant to grow with you. Use them regularly to add, remove, and reflect on what truly matters to you.

The process of evolving doesn't happen in a day, a week, or even a month. It takes time, sometimes months or even years. That's why these worksheets should stay active in your life. Your answers will keep changing as you gain new insights, face new challenges, and grow into the person you are meant to become.

## Master Your Goals

Almost everyone might be talking about goals or goal setting. I attended Growth Setting Mastery by Sensei, which was different from all the goal-setting programs. It was life-changing for me and my family, as well as for my fellow leaders who participated and practiced it.

It changed my mindset, perspective on life, behavior, and habits, and I began to reflect frequently on my vision. He insisted it is not about goals and achieving them. Grow beyond your goals by expanding your vision, which leads to ultimate joy and you can experience a default version of yourself. He taught me that you can achieve your goals, whereas you can't achieve your vision completely. This is because your vision should expand as you achieve your goals and grow.

Your vision needs to evolve based on your accomplishments and personal development. This means you should continuously enlarge your dreams and work towards them. In fact, your vision should evolve and expand as you get closer to it, always pushing you to new heights. Life is short, you can't give pause to your goals, and you need to grow beyond your goals.

When it comes to growth setting, some goals I have accomplished after setting goals are my international trip, buying my own home in India, moving to a different location in India, as well as in the UAE, becoming an author, sharing stages with great personalities, attending leading conferences and so forth.

Furthermore, I began attracting potential clients. People started reaching out, expressing interest in my coaching sessions. It is incredibly empowering!

My lifestyle has completely transformed since attending these sessions regularly. The guidance I received encourages me to prioritize growth over results. Are you ready to focus on your goals?

Often your goals are very meaningful to you and can have a lasting impact on your life. Remember, goals are not wishes.

Your goals must be like magnets. They pull you so strongly. That pull is so strong that you know how to say goodbye to your distraction, bring 180 to 189 existing pages, here, following the guidelines carefully.

## Challenges

In life, there are challenges. Life is a mixture of opportunities and challenges. I strongly believe what Helen Keller said is true, "Life is either a daring adventure or nothing at all."

I still remember when I was preparing slides on PowerPoint. My then 5-year-old son was there beside me. He was so curious to learn more about it. He slowly started experimenting and cried by asking why couldn't he type, and why couldn't he insert pictures, and his blame was many. I told him this is called a little challenge. You may feel these are big challenges. He asked what a challenge is. I told him it is very easy to understand, now you are a small boy. What do you do if you can't do something, for example, if you want to insert pictures on your slide, what did you do? You cried!

"Why did you cry?" I asked gently. He leaned toward me, his eyes wide with curiosity.

"You didn't know how to do it, right?" He nodded.

"That feeling you had, that's called a challenge." I smiled. "And you know what? Adults feel that way too. However, they often express it differently, through stress, frustration, or even anxiety. It's common."

He listened closely.

"See, for adults, so many things demand their attention, like paying the bills, managing work, taking care of the family. Life keeps moving, and they have to keep up, even when they feel stuck or overwhelmed."

I paused for a moment, then added, "So what you felt today? It's normal. The difference is, as we grow, we learn how to face our challenges, not avoid them. And that's exactly what you're learning now."

When you start something new, it feels hard. The next day, it gets a little easier. After a week, you might even enjoy it. That's how you and I grow bit by bit. He religiously agreed with this concept, because for him whatever, his mom, told him was correct. Now as a nine -year-old boy, though he still faces many challenges he can prepare his slides.

If you truly want to achieve your goal you need to be authentic to yourself. You need to be unstoppable. Take your failures as your stepping stones. Let your goal make you stretch so that you can transform into a better person of incredible dimensions, in your own eyes.

Goals challenge you to grow. Face your challenges along the way, and enjoy the process of getting things done. When you are on your journey toward growth, do not even think about perfection. Perfectionism is the enemy of success. No one is perfect in this world. Everyone has their flaws. During your journey, you can identify your flaws, strengths, and weaknesses. You make changes, according to what your course demands.

## Prioritize for Productivity

Always remember to prioritize your goals and tasks. The most important and toughest task should be done in the early hours, or during your most productive time. The productive time may be different for each person. However, if you use it well, little by little, you'll start achieving your goals.Action is the most important thing.

## Call to Action

Which of your goals seems riskier? Why? Thinking too much about the 'how' can feel overwhelming and may demotivate you. Instead, focus on the rewards you'll enjoy once you get there.

CHAPTER 24

# ASPECTS OF GOAL SETTING

*"People with goals succeed because they know where they're going."*

**– Earl Nightingale,**
**Author and pioneer of the self-help movement**

Within the pages of this chapter, you will discover the art of goal setting the profound journey of self-discovery and purposeful action. Through the prism of evaluation, reflection, and intention, you will chart a course toward your deepest desires, guided by the timeless principles of SMART goals.

## Dreams and Goals

As we mentioned earlier, I believe now you know your goals, and how to select. Whenever you set your goals or are working through Part II, you may refer back to Part I, and vice versa. Both parts are interconnected.

## SMART Goals

a) **Specific:** Your goals need to be clear, not vague. Not only for you but for others as well. If you ask your 5-year-old son to read aloud your goals, he must understand what you have written. That means your goals are as clear as even a 5-year-old child can understand. Be specific about what you want to achieve. Why? and How?

b) **Measurable:** Quantify your goal. Is there any measuring tool to know that you have achieved your goal?
Whether it is measured by hours, weeks, years, dollars, kilograms, kilometers, or some other scale, we must be able to measure it or experience it. A SMART goal is measurable.
How much/ how many?

________________________________________

________________________________________

________________________________________

________________________________________

c) **Achievable:** Be honest with yourself. Your goal must be doable. It doesn't mean that it is, or will be 'easy'. If you know how you are going to do, your goal is too small; there is no thrill in it. It must be challenging and at the same time achievable. You need to know where you are right now, physically, spiritually, emotionally, and knowledge-wise.
How can I achieve this goal?

________________________________________

d) **Realistic/Risky**: Set realistic goals. Your goals should be in line with your vision, and don't waste time with irrelevant goals that distract you from your actual purpose.
For one person, a goal may be realistic, but for another, it may be unrealistic. Everything depends upon where you are right now. Depends on your actuality. Does the goal align with your purpose? Yes, or no?
You must be ready to take a calculated risk.

e) **Timebound:** Set a deadline to achieve your goal, otherwise it is merely a dream. Or there might be a chance to procrastinate. Your mind will tempt you to keep it for tomorrow, that tomorrow will never come. You must have a timeline.
By when ----------------

### Accountability

It is good if someone is there to ask you frequently, about your goals, and motivate you. Otherwise, chances are that you might quit the goal. Having an accountability partner will boost your energy to do more.

When my mentor identified my strength, in writing, he popped into to his WhatsApp group and announced, in the group, that this is her strength, the area she is excellent at, and she is going to come up with her book soon. He told me, "Whenever you need any help concerning this goal, I am here." An accountability partner would be an inspiring person, who is very optimistic and supportive. You can share your wildest dreams with them. Experience it. You will feel good about it and will feel like, why didn't I have this idea earlier?

My friend, Muneer Amayoor, who wrote a book that became an Amazon best seller. The first thing he did was challenge himself. When he set his goal to write a book, he published its cover page on social media and kept accountability partners. Then people started asking him where his book was, and he pushed himself very hard to complete publishing it. I was fortunate to be his accountability partner by going through his script. He invited our family to be a part of his launch.

Accountability matters. This gives energy to both sides, meaning, to the goal-setter and the accountability partner. He has become my accountability partner in writing this book. With great attention to detail, he reviewed my manuscript and offered constructive feedback to strengthen both the content and structure. Beyond the writing process, he guided me on how to approach publishers effectively and shared strategic insights on aligning with, rather than merely following, their marketing approach. His support has been instrumental throughout this journey. In this regard, he has truly been a mentor to me.

What we discussed here is external accountability. Do you have any idea about internal accountability? You need great support from yourself. You judge yourself with honesty. Hold yourself accountable and own your mistakes. Anticipate challenges.

### Evaluate, Reflect, and Ponder

You need to evaluate your progress. Believe in the process. If you are not reaching your goal, evaluate what is happening, what went wrong, what went well, what you need to improve, and based on your current needs re-adjust your plans, and consistently work on it.

Revisit, redraw, and update your goals every now and then. Those who take the time to evaluate will find that they are like a deep-rooted tree in the desert, very strong! Because they build a strong foundation first, they know what went well and what did not.

Ask some self-reflective questions. All the clarity-related questions I explained in detail in my book, '101 Clarity Questions to Be in the Company of Clarity'

How will you integrate the principles of SMART goals into your goal-setting process? What steps will you take to ensure that your goals are SMART?

## SMART Milestone Goal-setting Statement

Let us take some examples of SMART milestone goal-setting statements. Model and modify, create your statement. Read it aloud every morning and evening. Create a small statement card, and make it your screen saver, wallpaper, and everywhere possible at your house.

## Goal Card

Write in a card

**My goal**

1. *By Month/Date/Year or sooner*

   I am so happy and grateful that, followed by a clear, emotionally compelling, present-tense description of your goal as if it's already achieved.

**Statement: More Examples**

2. Thank God and the universe. Today is the... date,... month, and... year and I am grateful that I have successfully **delivered** five speaking engagements at Expo City Dubai.

3. Thank God and the universe. Thrilled to be consistently exercising by participating in the Dubai Run 2023, two days a week, wearing a medium-sized top by... (date),... (month),... (year), or sooner.

4.

**THANK GOD**

**I am so happy and grateful that I have completed my book proposal and copy-edited chapters by ---- (date), --- (month), --- year), or sooner.**

*Signature:* __________

5. Thank God and the universe. I am so glad and grateful that I am putting all my knowledge, skills, and abilities into generating... amount by... (date), ... (month),... (year), or sooner, by doing (could be coaching, training, writing, marketing, investing) monthly... times (how many times) Money is coming to me regularly from multiple sources in increasing quantities.

### Call to Action

Share your goal card with your family. Create separate goal cards for different areas of your life. Keep them in your wallet, look at them often, read them aloud, and feel genuinely thrilled.

# CHAPTER 25

# WHY DON'T PEOPLE SET GOALS?

> *"To the person who does not know where he wants to go there is no favorable wind."*
>
> **– Seneca**
>
> **Stoic philosopher of ancient Rome**

In this chapter, let's explore why people don't set goals. The reasons are as varied as the individuals themselves, however, at the core, many are driven by fear, uncertainty, and distractions that prevent them from tapping into their true potential. For some, the thought of setting ambitious goals feels daunting—there's a fear of failure or the belief that they're simply not capable. Others may struggle with self-doubt or over thinking like, "I'm not ready," or "I'm not qualified enough." These limiting beliefs create mental barriers that keeps them from taking the first step.

Many are also caught in the cycle of instant gratification—chasing short-term pleasures like social media, parties, and distractions—sacrificing long-term fulfillment for momentary enjoyment. This mindset keeps them trapped in a comfort zone, where growth and progress seem like distant concepts.

However, the real reason people don't set goals often lies in a lack of clarity. Without a clear vision or understanding of where they want to go, it becomes easy to drift through life, reacting to circumstances rather than creating the future they desire. When people are tangled in distractions and emotions, they forget the power of intentional living and the freedom that comes with having a defined purpose. Even though they are overwhelmed due to distractions, they are not ready to change and sitting behind the fence, watching curiously what others are doing!

In this chapter, we'll dive deeper into the barriers that prevent people from setting meaningful goals and explore how shifting your mindset can unlock a path to success.

### 1. Ignorance of the Importance of Goal-setting

During my one-on-one coaching sessions with my clients, I usually ask them about their goals. Some are shocked to realize the fact that there is such a way to win. Some are ignorant about having a compelling, pulling goal.

Jim Rohn says, *"Don't just think it, ink it."*

People don't set goals because they write them in a negative statement. It is not going to work. Write it in a positive statement.

### 2. They Set Unrealistic Goals

During our coaching session, Sensei inquired about my target monthly income, and I ambitiously stated an unrealistic figure. Reflecting on this later, I realized that my overconfidence was influenced by my practice of Neurogym techniques by John Assaraf. I thought I could tell a huge amount because I was practicing Neurogym. I needed to set realistic goals based on where I was standing at that time. I totally ignored this part.

It's important to set achievable goals based on your current circumstances, allowing for gradual growth over time. Setting unrealistic targets can be demotivating and may even prevent you from taking action altogether.

### 3. There is no Time Frame

If you don't set a time frame, every day you may hear that little chit-chat, "Let me take some rest today, tomorrow I will do more."

A dream without a deadline is merely a fantasy, not a goal. Time frames, on the other hand, trigger a sense of accountability and urgency, pushing you to act. They create a sense of structure, helping the brain stay engaged with the goal and keeping you on track. The science of goal setting shows that when you commit to a specific timeline, your brain aligns its resources toward achieving the goal, resulting in more focused efforts and greater success.

### 4. Lack of Belief

Self-belief catalyzes effective goal-setting, influencing not only personal motivation but also the perception and support of others in the pursuit of those goals. Believing in yourself and your dreams is crucial; without that, it's challenging to expect others to believe in you. Self-belief lays the foundation for confidence and resilience. Remember, your unwavering faith in your abilities and aspirations not only motivates you but also inspires others to believe in your journey.

What is your belief about your finances? Do you feel like you're broke, or do you feel like you're a magnet for money? What is your belief about your lifestyle or relationships? Are you listening to those little voices saying, "I am not good enough"? Do you think, "I don't have time to pursue my passion after my 9-to-6 job"? If so, then that is your reality. Decide what beliefs you want to cultivate and understand that you are the captain of your ship.

### 5. Opinion of Others

You are more conscious of what others say. Others' reality is not your reality. You are shaped based on your childhood, the people around you, the environment you had, the type of parenting you had, the type of schooling you had, what you heard, and what you learned. You need to be your commander. Show them that they are wrong! Create your own stories.

As an accountable leader, you must set compelling goals to make your life meaningful.

## THE SKY IS NOT THE LIMIT, IT'S THE LAUNCHPAD

Clarity in your vision is essential for achieving your goals and making progress towards your aspirations. When you have a clear vision of what you want to achieve, you can focus your energy, time, and resources on the tasks and actions that will help you reach your objectives. If you have a clear vision, you are seeing the whole picture of your future life in different areas of your life.

> ***Vision is your broad life picture***

With clarity, you can set specific and measurable goals, establish priorities, and make decisions that align with your vision. This helps you stay on track, avoid distractions, and use your time and resources more wisely.

When you have a clear picture of what you want to achieve, it is easier to stay motivated and persist through the challenges and obstacles you encounter along the way. Having a clear vision also helps you to communicate your goals and aspirations to others and to get the support you need to achieve them. The clarity in your vision is crucial to achieving your short-term as well as long-term goals and making progress toward your aspirations.

It also helps you to get the support you need to achieve your goals and aspirations. Make sure to take the time to clearly define your vision and make it a priority, it will serve as a compass and guide you on your journey towards success.

When you have a clear vision, you get excited, you get charged, and motivated. There is no room for laziness. You feel a sense of urgency. You will not be tired of your existing job schedule, because you know, along with your job, that to run the show, you need to grow and achieve your personal goals. Goals are the keys to your growth.

Many people quit their grandest dream in the middle of the journey, and one strong reason is lack of clarity. Often, their dream is bigger than their current mindset, and they expect immediate results, forgetting the power of patience and the importance of consistent effort.

People leave their vision, in the middle or initial stage itself, because they always think about 'how' in context of where he/she is right now. Most people could only see small pictures in their minds and thus set small goals, which are easy to handle.

Never connect the goals you want to achieve with your history or your past failures. That will sabotage you.

Are you proud of the standard of living that you have? Or are you feeling guilty for not leading the life you want? Do limiting beliefs about your goals clutter your mindset? The Sky is Not the Limit, It's the Launchpad.

Let us look at the story of the UAE. It is because of imagination that many deserts in the Middle East became cities, with five-star or seven-star hotels. Imagination is your greatest asset; tap into it to bring more ideas.

I have observed the UAE setting goals for various sectors, spanning different timelines like 2026, 2030, and 2050, and 2070. These goals cover areas such as climate action, transportation mobility management, environmental vision, industrial strategy, water security, surface transport master plans, interplanetary missions, and hosting expos. We need to understand that it was a barren land just 60 years ago, and now, look at the massive power of vision. The UAE has already set its vision for the next 45 years and is striving relentlessly to achieve it. As Sheikh Mohammed bin Rashid Al Maktoum once said, “The future does not wait for those who hesitate. The future can be designed and built today.”

It became a hub of cultural diversity, due to the leaders’ great vision, dreams, ambitions, openness to new things, and striving for the best.

They didn’t even have their own currency. They used Indian currency. By collaborating, modeling, and modifying different countries’ ideas, encouraging the wildest imagination of youngsters and unstoppable actions.

Whenever I attend global forums or summits as a clarity coach, I ask one question to the leaders participating in these events: “How do you feel here?” Their response is always the same—they speak non-stop about the hospitality, food, culture, openness, and the freedom they experience in just a few days. The impact of their visit is clear, most of them decide to set up their business or buy property in the the UAE for frequent visits.

Until I met my mentor, I had not seriously thought about my life 30 years in the future. I believed I would live as life offers and put in some effort, there was no powerful imagination and no timeline. Now I am learning from the country, the UAE where I live, happily, holding my shoulder straight, because here I don't need to bother about what others think of me. I can work on my creativity, with nothing bothering me.

You must discard limiting beliefs such as "I am too old," "I am incompetent," "I am not good enough," and "I am not smart enough." "My spouse/parents/kids don't love me". "Nobody likes my conversation", "I can't earn the money that I set to" etc. Write down the limiting beliefs you ha

Most of our beliefs are not true. They are unreal. You can bring clarity on which stories you are telling yourself are true and which are not.

> ***When patience, practice, purpose, and passion align, they create the perfect formula for achieving your goals.***

**Strategic Plan**

> *"Always plan ahead. It wasn't raining when Noah built the ark."*
>
> – **Richard Cushing**

This thought explains the significance of a plan in your lives. No other words articulate the importance of strategic planning as effectively as this thought does. Let us look at the story of Luigi Cani, a world-renowned Brazilian skydiver, recently took a daring leap to address the critical issue of deforestation in the Amazon. Cani jumped from a plane over a deforested area of the rainforest, releasing 100 million seeds from 27 different tree species.

This incredible achievement was the result of five years of meticulous planning, securing permits, designing a special biodegradable box for the seeds, and transporting tons of equipment and a film crew to the Amazon. Each seed was hand-collected from nearby rainforests two months before the jump to ensure their viability.

Despite numerous challenges, including failed test boxes and personal injuries, Cani successfully released the seeds from approximately 6,000 feet above the ground. With an impressive germination rate of over 95%, these seeds are expected to grow into trees that can reach up to 50 meters in height. The full impact of this initiative will be monitored via satellite over the next two years.

Cani said, "I struggled to hold onto the box and nearly broke my wrist and fingers. I managed to stabilize myself at around 6,000 feet, and the seeds were released exactly where we wanted them. It was pure ecstasy."

> ***Who you become is shaped by your planning and actions, fueled by complete commitment.***

Cani continues to use his daring stunts for greater causes. Looking ahead, he plans a future jump focusing on ocean plastic. "I've been jumping for 25 years and always pushed the limits with risky jumps. Now, at 51, I no longer seek danger for its own sake. I want to do something meaningful. Just like the seed drop, this next project will have real significance.

### Route

Just like planning a trip, you need to map out your goals. Before you start your trip, ask some powerful questions to create your route toward your goal. The result is a better-defined goal that is built on the S.M.A.R.T. framework.

In Los Angeles, Travis Kalanick felt deeply frustrated, not because of failure, but because of a common everyday problem:

it was incredibly difficult to find a reliable cab when needed. This frustration turned into curiosity. "Why isn't there a better way to get from point A to point B?"

That simple question became the starting point of what would later become Uber, a global ride-hailing platform that redefined personal transportation.

Travis didn't just set a goal. He began crafting a route to make that goal real.

However, the route wasn't straight. It was a journey filled with:

Unpredictable turns, from fighting city transport regulations to facing legal pushbacks

Route recalculations, entering new cities, adjusting business models, changing leadership styles

Expansions, beyond rides, into food delivery (Uber Eats), and logistics (Uber Freight)

Each phase required course correction, vision, and clarity of direction, all the key elements of a well-defined route. Travis knew that without a solid route, even the most exciting destination could remain unreachable.

Setting goals is like having a map to reach your favorite place. It helps you find the best way easily, so you can enjoy the journey and get to where you want to go!

You need to understand that even if two people have the same goal, based on their reality, the route they take would be different, based on their productivity, speed, and where they are right now, based on their skills, and knowledge. Here, see Travis's mindset and commitment, he didn't stop at the idea. He stayed on course, adapted when needed, and kept refining the route until the destination became reality. His story reminds us that a goal without a route is just a wish. It's the clarity of direction, the mindset to stay focused, and the commitment to take consistent action that drives success.

Some may be slow to achieve things. Some may go faster than others. It is not about how you are going to achieve it; however, it is about the process and commitment you put. You must enjoy the process. You don't need to focus on your results. What have you learned through this journey?

## Call to Action

As a visioneer, can your team see and feel the vision through the way you lead, decide, and show up every day?

CHAPTER 26

# LEARN TO LOVE YOURSELF

*"Caring for your body, mind, and spirit is your greatest and grandest responsibility. It's about listening to the needs of your soul and then honoring them."*

**– Kristi Ling, Happiness strategist, transformational life and business coach**

When you are on your journey toward personal growth, many things can go wrong because this is a new way of being. You may be starting from scratch, and the path may not be smooth. Don't punish yourself when challenges arise. Don't stop there. Pause and analyze the situation carefully. Give yourself some time to breathe. It is your responsibility to be kind to yourself.

Self-care involves recognizing personal needs and taking deliberate actions to nurture oneself. In a fast-paced world, self-care is a crucial aspect of maintaining a healthy balance and preventing burnout.

It is a process of knowing yourself deeply, connecting with your inner self, overcoming limiting beliefs, letting go of everything that you can't control, and so forth. It is a matter of knowing and understanding yourself better.

List out the ten things that you did, in this month, whether big or small, no matter. Let us name your wins. In most cases, human beings forget to give importance to their small wins or big wins and become overwhelmed with the tasks and responsibilities we need to achieve.

Instead of focusing on the tasks to be achieved, or the pending tasks, take a pause and celebrate the little wins. That makes a huge impact on your life. Be clear about your wins. Be clear about your achievements.

When you achieve small wins regularly, it can help you build momentum and confidence, which can lead to even greater accomplishments.

One of the key benefits of daily wins is that they can help people stay motivated. This can be especially important when working on long-term projects or goals, as it can be easy to become demotivated or lose sight of the bigger picture.

Another benefit of daily wins is that they can help people develop better habits. When people make a habit of achieving small wins every day, it can help them build momentum and make it easier to maintain that habit over time. This can be especially important when working on habit-forming goals such as exercising more, eating healthier, or reducing stress.

Moreover, daily wins can also help people improve their productivity. When people have a sense of accomplishment and a sense of progress, it can help them focus better and become more efficient.

When you achieve small wins every day, it can help them build their confidence.

**Reflection**

- Write down, I am proud that I have set my healthier boundary ------, -----, ----------

Fill in the blanks with 10 different things.

- Write down ten things you admire about yourself. It could be your hair, eyes, and so on.
- Write a love letter to yourself. If you are feeling down, read this letter. You feel energised.
- Write down what rejuvenates you. How do you feel now?

Practicing self-care is a critical step towards success and abundance.

## Call to Action

How do you plan to incorporate self-care practices into your daily routine to nurture your body, mind, and spirit?

Recall a moment when everything went wrong, you couldn't control your emotions, and you thought everything was lost. A few hours later, you started following your intuition, which said, slow down. You have done an amazing job. Stop for a while, give yourself some time to breathe, and start over with a good vibe. Have you experienced this? If so, cherish that memory.

# CHAPTER 27

# ACHIEVING GOALS WITH THE RULE OF FIVE

*"A goal without a plan is only a dream."*

**– Brian Tracy**

Goals require consistency and a simple yet powerful strategy. In the world of successful authors, Jack Canfield and Mark Victor Hansen found their key to success in the rule of five. Let's explore how this rule transformed their dream of making Chicken Soup for the Soul a best-seller.

### The Rule of Five

Leaders Jack and Hansen aimed to create an impactful best-selling book. To navigate the overwhelming world of book marketing, they sought advice from successful authors and experts. The turning point came when Ron Scolastico shared a profound insight – the concept of taking five swings at a large tree every day until it falls. This marked the birth of the rule of five.

### Execution

They both committed to taking five specific actions daily to achieve their goal. They detailed this strategy in the rule of five, focusing on targeted efforts. In his book Success Principles, Canfield shares how they implemented the rule:

Sending five review copies to eager editors.

Contacting five network marketing companies to purchase books as motivational tools.

Conducting seminars for at least five people and selling the book.

Distributing five copies to celebrities like Harrison Ford, Steven Spielberg, and Sidney Poitier.

### Consistency and Effort

To achieve their dream, leaders jack and Hansen tirelessly executed their plan. They made phone calls, wrote press releases, appeared on talk shows at odd hours, gave talks in churches, and even convinced gas stations, restaurants, and bakeries to sell their book. Despite the challenges, they remained consistent and committed.

### Results

The journey to success was not instant. It took a year of persistent effort for Chicken Soup for the Soul to hit the best-seller list. The rule of five played a crucial role in their achievement, proving that consistency, focus, commitment, concentration, and competency are essential elements in reaching goals.

### Application to Your Life

To apply the rule of five to your life, identify five specific actions that align with your goals. Create a plan, stay consistent, and embrace the journey. Whether it's sending emails, making calls, or networking, focus on five impactful actions daily. Remember, success may not happen overnight, however, with dedication, it's achievable.

This rule, as shown by by these leaders, offers a simple yet effective approach to achieving goals. By embracing consistency and focusing on five specific actions, you can pave your way to success. Apply this rule to your life, stay committed, and witness the transformation of your dreams into reality.

## Call to Action

Look at your goal as one of the biggest trees/rocks you have ever seen in your life. (Consider the one that resonates with you the most)

Treat your goal as if you were to go to this tree/rock with your powerful tool, every single day as mentioned in the rule of five. What will happen? With commitment, consistency, and the power of one (focus on one thing at a time) you will conquer it! What are the five specific actions you can take every day to conquer it? Write them down and start today. How will you use the Rule of five to transform your dreams into reality?

## CHAPTER 28

# THINGS THAT AFFECT PEOPLE

*"Watch every detail that affects the accuracy of your work."*

**– Arthur C. Nielsen,**
**A market research pioneer**

The human experience is shaped by a lot of interconnected factors that influence individuals at physical, emotional, and social levels. External elements such as culture, environment, and socioeconomic status also play pivotal roles in shaping a person's perspectives and opportunities.

Relationships, both familial and social, significantly impact one's sense of belonging and well-being. Ultimately, the dynamic interplay of these elements contributes to the rich and diverse nature of the human experience.

Let us discuss. We need to have clarity on all these five factors, to become the best version of ourselves. Clear thoughts and awareness make you a better person.

- **The Environment**

As a visionary person, you must know about your environment to thrive. Evaluate your current environments, including your home, work, and relationships, to determine if they align with your aspirations of being the best in the world at what you do. If they do not, take proactive steps to detach yourself from those environments and seek ones that support your goals and growth. You must surround yourself with people who see greatness in you.

Another thing you need to think about is your contribution to the environment. You and I need to contribute something to our environment. It could be carrying a water bottle to reduce the number of plastic bottles on the planet. Caring is the one thing we need to practice as a social being. By setting goals, by taking responsibility for a sustainable environment, we can make the world a better place to live for us as well as the next generation. Help others with your purpose. Consider various ways you can contribute to the society. Whether through sharing your skills, supporting causes close to your heart, or volunteering your time, every effort counts. Reflect on how your unique abilities and passions can make a positive impact on the lives of others. Sometimes, even small gestures can create lasting change.

- **Events**

Every day you face many events. What are you experiencing right now? That is an event for you. It could be, big, small, local, national, or of global significance.

- **Knowledge**

Confucius (551–479 BCE) opined, "Education breeds confidence. Confidence breeds hope. Hope breeds peace."

He emphasized lifelong learning, self-cultivation, and moral education as key to a harmonious society.

Every day you learn. What you don't know will tragically affect you. It leads to emptiness in your life. Daily read something that depends on your goal. If you read things that are aligned with your purpose, your journey will be easy. Learn every day. Enroll in a course, to gain knowledge.

During your journey, you need to unlearn many things that are not going to serve you. And remember to relearn things that are going to serve you to achieve your goals, or that are aligned with your values.

You are no longer in the industrial age. You live in an era where you have the freedom to choose what you learn and how you learn it. However, distractions are at their peak. This is where clarity becomes your compass, helping you focus, filter out the noise, and navigate toward the right subject or the right platform for self-learning.

- **Result**

Whether you do something, or you don't do something, you will get the result. You are affected by the result. If you build some good habits and follow disciplines, by taking action you are going to get the result you wanted.

- **The Dream**

Clarity turns dreams into goals, and goals into reality. A dream backed by clarity, focus, and action becomes a tangible success. You need to understand that the pull of the future must be greater than the pull of the past. I see mediocre people live in the past, by discussing their past follies, mistakes, and jokes. What is the use, if you are not using mistakes as a stepping ladder? I could see many WhatsApp groups, sucking other's time by simply discussing past experiences.

They lament over small things and forget to live in the present. The only thing you can control is your present activities. If you are part of such a mediocre group, stop reading this page immediately and leave that group. Such places are not for you.

Average people tend to dream small, lacking the courage to dream big; they believe that thinking big is the right or privilege of peak performers.

## Call to Action

Reflect on the factors that shape your human experience, physical, emotional, social, cultural, environmental, and socioeconomic. Choose one factor and brainstorm practical actions you can take to positively impact it.

CHAPTER 29

# BUCKET LIST

*"A bucket list is an invitation to dream bigger"*

**– Annette White,**

**Author of Bucket List Adventures**

"Let us exchange our minds one day so that I too can dream like you," Rasheed often tells me. I dream a lot, not only in my sleep but also during the day. I dream about visiting many places, the life I want, and the recognition I would love to receive for my achievements, amount of money I want to earn and invest. At night, I even dreamed of being an astronaut as I lay on my pillow, that was a fantasy!

I believe you all dream a lot like me.Many years ago, while visiting Dubai's largest mall, I came across a beautifully designed journal with an eye-catching title, "Bucket List." The phrase intrigued me, as it was a new concept to me at the time. I wondered, why call it a bucket list?

Curious, I began researching and soon discovered its powerful meaning. A bucket list is a collection of experiences and goals one hopes to accomplish in a lifetime. It's more than just a list; it's a personal roadmap to making dreams a reality.

As I delved deeper, I discovered the story behind the term. It all started with two hospital roommates, both diagnosed with incurable diseases. One of them, Carter, was a humble mechanic who began writing a list of everything he wanted to do before he died. At first, he dismissed it as impossible. However, when his wealthy roommate, Edward, found it is impactful and interesting, unlike Carter, Edward had the financial means to turn dreams into reality. Despite their challenges, they set out on an extraordinary journey, making the list come to life.

This story was later captured in the movie The Bucket List (2007), starring Jack Nicholson and Morgan Freeman. The film beautifully portrays how embracing adventure, friendship, and purpose can transform the final chapter of life into something truly meaningful.

So, if you got inspired, take a moment to write your own bucket list. Let it be deeply personal, filled with things that excite and inspire you. After all, life is too precious to leave dreams unfulfilled.

There is nothing wrong in daydreaming, however, it is your call, to hold those dreams to lead a fulfilling life. To do that bucket list will help you, and setting goals will help you, not only just set the goals, but also you need to take small actionable steps.

To understand the term "bucket list," you need to know about your dreams. Dream, dream, dream, and before they fade away, write, write, write.

What are the things you're truly interested in and passionate about? Based on your passion and purpose, the values and goals you decide. Like:

- Health
- Wealth
- Career/Business
- Family
- Friends

- Unique Experiences
- Food
- Hobbies
- Skills

One example: Write about 50 places you want to visit before you die. This will give you the momentum to lead a colorful life. Start with your 'biggest why', not with 'how can I can do, or make money'. Refer back to the Goal Setting chapter for more details. You need to believe it first to achieve it. If you have clarity, it is like an arrow, you will hit the bull's eye.

Most of the successful leaders said that they had no idea about how to achieve their wildest dreams. A great leader said when he wrote 'I am a brilliant and savvy businessman', he didn't believe it, not one bit, then he designed that new belief into his brain.

If you want to know more about bucket lists, read books like. "500 Things to Do Before You Kick the Bucket" written by

Donald Vaughan, Christine A. Dallman and Christine Halvorson

Let me share some examples of bucket lists

- Take an International Trip to Malaysia with my mom and dad (date)
- Shoot an interview with my mentor and great leaders. Continue my interview podcast series.
- Visit a tropical island
- Climb the Himalayas
- Work from a resort hotel
- Start my own business
- Invest in real estate
- Invest in digital gold
- Donate Dirhams, 10,000 every year

- Plant 500 trees in my plot, and 100 trees on the street
- Stay in the Amazon Rainforest for a week
- Trek to Machu Picchu
- Go on a cruise ship
- Fly in a private jet
- Snorkeling in Dubai Aquarium
- Shake hands with H.H Sheikh Mohammed, Bin Rashid Al Maktoum

For all your goals keep a timeline. Approximate years, months you will take to achieve it. Start writing yours.

### Six Ways to Get Started with Your Bucket List

1. Express gratitude for both your achievements and the goals you have yet to reach. This practice will elevate your mindset, fostering growth and a higher level of awareness.
2. Make a long list of everything you've achieved, big or small. It's proof that you're already a champion, just to encourage yourself. This is called reverse bucket list. The idea is to help you realize that you've done more than you think. It's a great way to be thankful for those experiences, rather than frustrated at the things we haven't done.
   Now make a long list of what you want to achieve or experience, don't hold back. Then, using the Clarity Wheel as your guide, narrow it down. Choose the ten that matter most to you from each category.
3. Organize based on the time frame. This week, this month, this year, three years, five years, ten years, and 25 years, like how you did for the goal setting.

4. Make a list of things you're unhappy with, currently in your life, which helps you address those issues and understand your passions, guiding you in creating a meaningful bucket list.
5. Talk to your best friend or family about creating your list together.
6. Publish it online, then kickstart with steps and strategies.

**Call to Action**

What's the first item you're adding to your bucket list? Take a moment to reflect on your passions, values, and dreams, then write down 50 things you're truly excited about experiencing or achieving in your lifetime. I challenge you to share it on social media to hold yourself accountable.

CHAPTER 30

# INTENTIONS, ACTIONS, TRANSFORMATION: AIM HIGHER, GROW STRONGER

*"The man who moves a mountain begins by carrying away small stones."*

**– Confucius,**
**Ancient Chinese philosopher**

Goal-setting is a powerful tool for achieving personal growth. Goals serve as benchmarks for progress, pushing individuals beyond their comfort zones and facilitating continuous learning. As individuals work towards achieving their goals, they often acquire new skills, overcome challenges, and develop a deeper understanding of themselves; thus, they grow through the process. It is a journey. Once you achieve one goal, you are not going to stop there, right? You need to grow in different aspects of your life, not just in one single direction. It's like needing to align your focus with all areas of life.

Let me share my growth journey briefly. When I discussed my grand vision with my mentor, he helped me identify my strengths and asked me to focus on them. Alongside, to enhance my strengths, I got specialized in speaking and presentation mastery, clarity coaching, and leadership empowerment courses.

Initially, breaking out of my comfort zone was challenging, and I faced many obstacles in learning these skills. Speaking in front of the camera was scary to me. I started using teleprompters to avoid my nervousness so that I thought I could see my scripts. It's funny now, looking back at that video after all these years. It was too tough to stand in front of the camera and speak, however, after one month of practice, I got to know how to present myself. Then slowly get into the clarity coaching field.

When I came to know more about coaching, I discovered one of my passions. I was passionately ready to learn the art of clarity coaching. However there too, it is not as easy as I thought. I needed to find out my clients, and for that, I needed to present myself. I knew I needed to create my fliers. I needed to market myself. I was reluctant to do that, however, so thrilled to bring clarity to others' lives. I felt it was fun to do. I faced challenges to make people understand the difference between coaching, counseling, and training. Most of the people thought it was some kind of training.

Challenges were there to find my potential clients. It was riskier. It was really hard to ask for money, once I met my clients, for my services. All are looking for free services, no matter what it is worth.

However, this journey ultimately led to my growth, and definitely, there is no full stop for the growth. It is an ongoing process filled with a hunger for learning new things and adapting to the changes happening in the world around you.

Be a transformer of your dreams, goals, and vision into reality. What is your next plan and, after that? And again after? Like life is a journey, you must move on to your vision based on your purpose and your strong values. That is called growth. Be ready to grow with your goals.

You grow only by facing challenges and by sticking to your biggest "why.". You grow only when you are ready to change. You grow only if you are ready to face adversity, or if you embrace failures.

Failure may punch you in the gut. Leaving you with throbbing wounds, and you may be stuck there. You have immense potential to bounce back. If you go through successful stories, every successful person, travelled through many faces of life, and gradually they reach the top, and they don't stop there. They are committed to expanding their vision to serve millions. Take the examples of leadership gurus like Jack Canfield, Lisa Nicols, Brian Tracy, Oprah Winfrey, Tony Robbins and many more. They faced innumerable challenges; however, they stand tall in front of us, because of the lessons they learned from their life.

It is said that once a group of astronauts, after achieving their biggest goal, had no idea what was next, a few of them went into depression. Why? They failed to set goals after their grand vision. Until your last breath, you need to have dreams, goals, and vision. For some after retirement, they simply live. You can make your retirement years livelier by participating in different activities based on your passion and purpose.

You all know that life does not get better by accident. Growth and transformation happen when you stretch towards your goal because you continually work on your knowledge and skills; thus, you grow.

What is next after achieving your goal?

Now that you've reached one of your goals, or are walking toward it, ask yourself:

"How will I continue to grow beyond this point?"

How will I measure my growth, not just by milestones, but by mindset?

Take a moment to reflect on all the puzzle pieces you've explored throughout this journey, values, intention, purpose, habits, action and mindset.

As we wrap up, remember, goal setting is like a puzzle. It's about the process of fitting, realigning, and learning. Embrace the journey. Celebrate the small wins. Grow through the storms. You are the artist and the architect of your life. This isn't the end, it's your next beginning.

### Call to Action

Write a letter to your 'self', about your transformational journey. Remember to start with gratitude.

# CHAPTER 31

# CONCLUSION: OWN YOUR CLARITY

> ***"Clarity is a call to ignite and a mirror so true—a quiet call from within that helps you glow. It awakens the power already in you."***

As you complete reading the Clarity Call, congratulations. You didn't just finish a book. You answered a deeper call. A call to be more intentional. A call to live with purpose. A call to meet yourself with honesty, empathy, love, and power.

It's clear that you carry a grand vision. You've dared to go inward. You've unpacked layers. You've listened to your inner voice.

So, let me ask you something before we part ways: Has your inner compass found its crystal clarity? How did the journey to your truest self unfold?

What are the changes you've made since the moment you picked up this book? I hope you've now taken committed steps toward your vision.

Pause for a moment and rate yourself, from the day you bought this book to this very moment of reflection.

Are you smiling right now? If you are, that means something beautiful has shifted. You've touched a new version of yourself, one that walks with compassion and live focussed.

When most people are asked, 'What's next?', they pause. But not you. You now know how to deconstruct the false reality imposed by others. You have seen that life lived on someone else's terms is not truly lived.

You've chosen discipline, not as a restriction, but as a path to peace.

You now understand the true power you hold, your mind, your awareness, your clarity.

You have the most powerful machine within you, your brain. Protect it like a sacred temple. Shield it with intention. You already know what deserves space inside and what doesn't.

Upgrading is always possible. Educate yourself. Reflect often. Spend time alone. Date yourself. Be your own greatest ally. And when life feels foggy again, because it will, don't panic. Just pause. Make the clarity call. Talk to yourself. It's not a one-time act. It's a habit. A lifestyle. A quiet revolution.

Let me know how you're doing. I'll be right here if you ever need a conversation for more clarity. I walk this path with you. Thank you from the bottom of my heart.

**Ready | Clear | Aligned | Let's Go**

You've already taken the first steps.
You've started shifting, growing, choosing differently.
However, growth isn't always linear.
When momentum dips, or doubt creeps in, I'm here.
Let's turn your clarity into consistency.
Let's fuel your next big move, together.

**For the Times When:**

✔ You feel overwhelmed or stuck mid-way
✔ You're ready to rise but unsure how
✔ You need a clear strategy and strong mindset
Book your private session now
Available online or face-to-face, globally

hello.ami.ras@gmail.com
www.linkedin.com/in/ami-rasheed-b447b420
971559691554